Medieval Knights and Warriors

Medieval Knights and Warriors

Other Books in the History Makers series:

Medieval Knights and Warriors

By Janet R. Zohorsky

LUCENT
BOOKS®

THOMSON
━━━━━✦━━━━━ ™
GALE

San Diego • Detroit • New York • San Francisco • Cleveland
New Haven, Conn. • Waterville, Maine • London • Munich

© 2003 by Lucent Books. Lucent Books is an imprint of The Gale Group, Inc.,
a division of Thomson Learning, Inc.

Lucent Books® and Thomson Learning™ are trademarks used herein under license.

For more information, contact
Lucent Books
27500 Drake Rd.
Farmington Hills, MI 48331-3535
Or you can visit our Internet site at http://www.gale.com

LIBRARY OF CONGRESS CATALOGING-IN-PUBLICATION DATA

Zohorsky, Janet R.
    Medieval knights and warriors / by Janet R. Zohorsky.
        p.   cm. — (History makers series)
Includes bibliographical references and index.
    ISBN 1-56006-954-6 (hardback : alk. paper)
    1. Knights and knighthood—Juvenile literature. 2. Middle Ages—
Juvenile literature. 3. Civilization, Medieval—Juvenile literature.
I. Title. II. History makers.
    CR4513 .Z64 2003
    940.1—dc21

                                                        2002007175

Printed in the United States of America

CONTENTS

FOREWORD

The literary form most often referred to as "multiple biography" was perfected in the first century A.D. by Plutarch, a perceptive and talented moralist and historian who hailed from the small town of Chaeronea in central Greece. His most famous work, *Parallel Lives*, consists of a long series of biographies of noteworthy ancient Greek and Roman statesmen and military leaders. Frequently, Plutarch compares a famous Greek to a famous Roman, pointing out similarities in personality and achievements. These expertly constructed and very readable tracts provided later historians and others, including playwrights like Shakespeare, with priceless information about prominent ancient personages and also inspired new generations of writers to tackle the multiple biography genre.

The Lucent History Makers series proudly carries on the venerable tradition handed down from Plutarch. Each volume in the series consists of a set of five to eight biographies of important and influential historical figures who were linked together by a common factor. In *Rulers of Ancient Rome*, for example, all the figures were generals, consuls, or emperors of either the Roman Republic or Empire; while the subjects of *Fighters Against American Slavery*, though they lived in different places and times, all shared the same goal, namely the eradication of human servitude. Mindful that politicians and military leaders are not (and never have been) the only people who shape the course of history, the editors of the series have also included representatives from a wide range of endeavors, including scientists, artists, writers, philosophers, religious leaders, and sports figures.

Each book is intended to give a range of figures—some well known, others less known; some who made a great impact on history, others who made only a small impact. For instance, by making Columbus's initial voyage possible, Spain's Queen Isabella I, featured in *Women Leaders of Nations*, helped to open up the New World to exploration and exploitation by the European powers. Inarguably, therefore, she made a major contribution to a series of events that had momentous consequences for the entire world. By contrast, Catherine II, the eighteenth-century Russian queen, and Golda Meir, the modern Israeli prime minister, did not play roles of global impact; however, their policies and actions significantly influenced the historical development of both their own countries and their regional neighbors. Regardless of their relative importance in the greater historical scheme, all of the figures chronicled in the History Makers series made contributions to posterity; and their public achievements, as well as what is known about their private lives, are presented and evaluated in light of the most recent scholarship.

In addition, each volume in the series is documented and substantiated by a wide array of primary and secondary source quotations. The primary source quotes enliven the text by presenting eyewitness views of the times and culture in which each history maker lived; while the secondary source quotes, taken from the works of respected modern scholars, offer expert elaboration and/or critical commentary. Each quote is footnoted, demonstrating to the reader exactly where biographers find their information. The footnotes also provide the reader with the means of conducting additional research. Finally, to further guide and illuminate readers, each volume in the series features photographs, two bibliographies, and a comprehensive index.

The History Makers series provides both students engaged in research and more casual readers with informative, enlightening, and entertaining overviews of individuals from a variety of circumstances, professions, and backgrounds. No doubt all of them, whether loved or hated, benevolent or cruel, constructive or destructive, will remain endlessly fascinating to each new generation seeking to identify the forces that shaped their world.

INTRODUCTION

The medieval knight was a warrior in a turbulent period of history. The Middle Ages, which spanned roughly A.D. 300 to 1500, began after the fall of the Roman Empire and ended with the Renaissance. It was a period of turmoil, violent invasion, and anarchy. The warrior of the Early Middle Ages (300–1066) behaved like a barbarian, but his role became a more honorable one during the medieval period (1067–1250) as he evolved into the armored knight on horseback with a code of moral values.

In order to emerge from the anarchy of the Early Middle Ages and build cities and civilizations, medieval society recruited the warrior to defend new towns and maintain order. However, since the warrior by definition is violent, he needed to be controlled, or inspired to devote himself to a lord, if he was to be trustworthy. Marrying a violent character by nature to peaceful objectives may seem like a melding of irreconcilable opposites. But it was a marriage of necessity. Medieval society had to convince the warrior that if he was going to fight and kill, he must perform his duty within the framework of a feudal society and the church. As a reward, his violent soul would be saved. The church became involved in the knighting ceremony, with swords viewed as miniature versions of the cross. The newly appointed knight was expected to adhere to a sophisticated system of values called the "code of chivalry," which included personal integrity, generosity, compassion, courtliness, loyalty, and prowess.

The medieval knight was charged with maintaining order in European society during a period of relative chaos.

BAYARD.

This new code of behavior continued to be refined throughout the eleventh and twelfth centuries until it was formalized in 1275 by Ramon Llull, a scholar deeply devoted to Christianity. The son of a celebrated Spanish knight, Llull spent fifty years traveling and studying religion and wrote many books on the subject. As the author of the first book on knighthood, called the *Book of the Order of Chivalry* (*Libre de l'Orde de Cavalleria*), Llull clearly defined the code of chivalry by which knights should live. A knight should first

> defend his faith and protect the Holy Church, second . . . defend his lord and protect the weak including women, widows and orphans . . . keep himself ready for action by continuous exercise by attending jousts and tournaments . . . accept office in secular government if the king chooses him, and he should act as judge or magistrate in local justice courts . . . [and] it is his duty to pursue criminals and bring them to justice.[1]

Richard the Lionheart, who served as the king of England for ten years, was a warrior who proudly led a Crusade against Muslims who had taken the Holy Land, believing there could be no greater glory than to eliminate the infidels. Religion also roused the Muslim leader Saladin to fight for the same land. Both men were outstanding and inspiring warriors to their own people.

Knighthood offered other, more earthly rewards than eternal life. It also allowed a person to better his economic status. In a feudal society, in which the knight protected his lord and lands, the knight was granted land in return for his services. Land ownership gave knights the opportunity to enter a new ruling class, which would allow them to take a role in governing society instead of just fighting for it. Knights dominated town councils as well as protected them. In subsequent decades when lords ran out of land to give knights, they granted money fiefs instead, providing knights with a source of money to support their expensive arms.

Although it was easier for men from the privileged classes to become knights, since they had the wealth to pay for costly equipment, it was not a prerequisite. William Marshal, Don Pero Niño, Bertrand du Guesclin, and John de Hawkwood are four knights who rose from relative poverty to fame and success. These individuals' exceptional abilities helped them overcome their disadvantages. However, while Marshal and Pero Niño embodied chivalrous behavior, Guesclin and Hawkwood resorted to more violent tactics, with little heed for honor, in pursuit of greater fortune.

Richard the Lionheart leads crusaders into battle against Saladin's Muslim warriors at Arsuf in 1191.

The values of Guesclin and Hawkwood were partly a product of the later medieval time in which they lived (1250–1500); knights eventually became a liability to kings, serving the nobility a little too faithfully. Kings desired more control and began to raise their own armies with new weapons and war tactics. The feudal system, a land-based economic system, slowly transformed into a monetary economic system, and nobles came to rely on mercenaries. Many knights no longer wished to provide so many days of battle service to their lords anyway, preferring to tend to their own manors and lives. But for those who wished to fight, the mercenary business became increasingly popular. In fact, Hawkwood led the most famous mercenary group, called the White Company. Both Hawkwood and Guesclin died as national heroes, but they were more unscrupulous mercenaries than ideal knights.

The reality of the medieval knight's life was that knighthood was a difficult profession. Success did not come instantly or sometimes at all, and simply staying alive was the greatest challenge most knights faced. Chivalry was an ideal to which knights aspired, but often fell short. Yet despite their very human weaknesses, knighthood implied an adherence to higher standards. Marshal, Richard I, Saladin, Don Pero Niño, Guesclin, and Hawkwood all in one way or another embodied some aspect of the notion of what a knight should be.

CHAPTER 1

The Medieval Knight and His World

The year 1066 ended the Early Middle Ages in England with the introduction of an economic system called feudalism. That year, Duke William of Normandy (from France), who came to be known as "William the Conqueror," invaded England. In defeating King Harold, the last in the line of Danish rulers, William changed the course of government from anarchy to an organized and efficient feudal order, and linked England with Western Europe instead of Scandinavia.

William introduced the feudal system (from the Latin word *feudum*, meaning "land held by military service") to England because he needed an effective way to rule his new kingdom. A king cannot be everywhere at once, so to control the vast lands, he spread his nobles around, and he rewarded each noble with land to oversee and from which to profit. A smart king was careful not to give a noble too much land in the same region to prevent the noble from becoming too powerful and rising up against the king. The price for this land was, first and foremost, loyalty to the king. Loyalty could translate into many tangible things, such as providing soldiers and paying money to the king.

Once the king's trusted nobles (counts, earls, dukes, and barons) were in place, the nobles recruited warriors to defend their lands against the four to five thousand Anglo-Saxons still living there. Since money was scarce in the eleventh century, paying warriors for their services was unrealistic. What William had in abundance, however, was land. So, he mandated that each noble could have a certain number of knights that would serve as his protection (as well as the king's, should he require an army). In return, each knight was to receive a piece of land, known as a fief (pronounced "fee"). Some knights paid shield money or a scutage (fee) to their lord if they did not wish to serve in a military capacity. The lord could then use the money to hire another knight in his place.

William the Conqueror leads Norman invaders at the Battle of Hastings,
where he defeated Harold II to become king of England.

The fiefs were farmed by peasants, many of them Anglo-Saxons.
Their labor produced crops and livestock for the knight to sell or
keep for his own household. A fief could also be anything that
generated income, such as a mill. If no land happened to be available, a noble could give his knight a money fief to support his
livelihood. By the end of the twelfth century, knights ran most of
the land. The land was well-used, protected, and profitable.

A pyramid of power, loyalty, and service, feudalism provided distinct roles and expectations for everyone. Nobles reported to the king, providing military services when required; knights owed allegiance to the nobles; and peasants farmed the lands and ran the mills for everyone's benefit. In this hierarchy, a man above another was called a lord, while a man below was a vassal. The knight was a vassal to a noble and a lord to his peasants.

Knights benefited the most from this new system of feudalism because it elevated their status from that of a soldier to that of a landowner. Along with this new status came responsibility. In governing his fief, a knight meted out justice among his peasants and officiated at events. And instead of being a full-time warrior, he served his lord only forty days each year. Sometimes, a knight would be named lord of a village, and he was often given a manor house in which to live.

Peasants, who made up the vast majority of the people, fared the worst in this system. The original Anglo-Saxons who lost all of their lands to William the Conqueror had to pay their new lords for the right to farm the land. In addition, they were obliged to provide their lord with crops as he desired and to defer to him for justice. As a result, generations of peasants remained poor, working the land without any real power. The largest benefit such a vassal received was the protection offered by his lord.

The key problem of feudalism stemmed from the granting of land in exchange for services: In time, all the land would be owned. In fact, by the thirteenth century there were more knights than fiefs. Also contributing to the diminished supply of land was the law of primogeniture. That is, a fief could not be divided among a knight's offspring upon his death; it could only be inherited in its entirety by a knight's eldest son. Therefore, if a man had six sons, only one was secured a stable future. (If a knight had only daughters, the fief would be given back to the lord to dispose of as he wished.) Eventually, an abundance of young men without land who needed to earn a living gave rise to mercenary knights, knights who were willing to fight for anybody's cause for pay.

The feudal system, therefore, eventually gave way to new economic systems. Once all of the land was divided up, future generations had no incentive to remain loyal to a noble or a king. An economic system in which soldiers were paid for loyalty replaced the feudal one.

On the Path to Knighthood

The path to becoming a knight was a stage that spanned many years. A preadolescent boy first became a page, then graduated to a

In the feudal system, a knight pledged loyalty and military service to a lord in exchange for land and power.

squire in his teenage years, and finally was dubbed a knight as a young man. Theoretically, a candidate for knighthood could be from either nobility or the common people, but, realistically, the process of becoming and outfitting a knight was very expensive. The wealthier a young man's family, the easier it was for a new knight to succeed.

A prospective knight's early years were spent in his own household, where he was taught good manners and courtesy. As early as seven years old, but more often ten, he would be sent away to another, grander household to train and serve as a page. Here, he would serve his elders meals, much like a waiter; he would learn to sing to entertain others; and he would learn basic falconry and hunting. Most important to his future as a knight, a page spent years learning the skills required for battle: how to care for and ride horses; use various weapons such as the sword, lance, mace, and ax; and wear armor.

Around the age of fourteen, a page would graduate to the status of a squire. A squire was assigned to a knight to serve as the knight's aide and companion. During the course of this close relationship, the squire was able to learn all he needed to know about becoming a knight by observing his master. He was responsible for the care of his master's armor and horse, as well as his master's comfort. The squire acted as a servant to his knight, which was an important characteristic of the knight himself in his life of loyal service to others. The squire also perfected his own military skills during this time. Sometimes, if his master was called to war, a sufficiently trained squire might even participate in the battle. However, most often, he was an observer. Nevertheless, witnessing battles provided the squire with the opportunity to understand what was demanded of a knight.

The squire continued to embrace the good manners and courtesy instilled in him from early childhood, expanding his knowledge to the knight's code of chivalry. This code promoted personal integrity, generosity, compassion, courtliness, loyalty, and prowess. In the feudal system, loyalty was a crucial element of the knight's identity. Without loyalty to his lord, the relationship would fail.

When a squire demonstrated sufficient mastery of all the knightly skills, he could be dubbed a knight. There was not a fixed time when this occurred. Often, as in William Marshal's case, it happened when his lord was in dire need of knights.

Arming a Knight

Even if a new knight demonstrated all of the abilities required for the job, he could not live his life as a knight if he lacked the proper equipment, which was costly. At a minimum, a knight required armor, a full set of weapons, and a strong warhorse. Ideally, he should have several horses, each for a different purpose.

Knights of the twelfth century, like William Marshal and Richard the Lionheart, wore a hauberk (chain-mail shirt), a coif (chain-mail hood), chausses (chain-mail leggings), a helmet, and a surcoat (a tunic worn over the hauberk to prevent it from rusting in wet weather). Chain mail was made from thousands of interlocking iron or steel rings, and it was intended to offer protection from an enemy's weapons. However, arrows shot from a longbow could easily penetrate chain mail's many holes. The average hauberk weighed twenty pounds. It cost one pound at the end of the twelfth century, and six pounds fifty years later.

By the thirteenth century, plate armor had been developed to better protect the knight. Made of iron or steel, plate-armor pieces fit over chain mail to protect the arms, elbows, legs, knees, feet, and torso. Plate armor was fastened on with straps, and it was the squire's job to help dress the knight for battle. By the time of Don

Pero Niño and Bertrand du Guesclin in the fourteenth century, knights still wore a combination of mail and plate, but plate armor was becoming more popular. The combined weight of these two types of armor made it burdensome and difficult for a knight who fell or was knocked from his horse.

The knight's primary weapon was the sword, made of a hilt (handle) and a blade. Medieval swords were made of iron and could be two and a half feet long and weigh three pounds. A lance was an essential weapon for the knight's cavalry charge. Armed with this wooden twelve-foot spear and charging at his enemy, a knight could cause serious damage or death. However, once the lance was used, it was difficult to retrieve even if it was still intact, so the knight needed other weapons to fall back on.

Some knights used a mace, which was a club reinforced with metal spikes on its head. A short-handled battle-ax also came in handy. Wielded by a knight on horseback, both of these weapons could smash through an enemy's helmet. If no other weapons were available, a knight used a dagger (a knife).

Since the main difference between a foot soldier and a knight was that the knight rode a horse, his horse was the knight's most important possession. (The French word for knight is *chevalier*, whose root word, *cheval*, means "horse.") A knight's success as a soldier was dependent on his horse. Medieval historian Andrea Hopkins notes that "the technique of charging [on horseback] with couched lance . . . was a revolutionary development and became the standard technique of medieval cavalry. . . . A whole line of knights charging in this manner seemed . . . to be unstoppable."[2]

The destrier (warhorse) that a knight rode into battle was a specific breed imported from France, Spain, and Turkey. It was strong, large, and reliable in the turmoil of battle. In addition, the knight needed a palfrey (a saddle horse) and might have other horses to carry his baggage and armor. A destrier was a knight's greatest expense. In the twelfth century, a destrier cost between two and six pounds, five times the price of a good cow. Even a palfrey cost between three and six pounds. By the end of the thirteenth century, a good destrier cost between ten and sixty pounds. The average knight earned less than one hundred pounds per year at that time. So, if his horse died in battle, it meant a tremendous financial loss.

Even with a warhorse, good weapons, and armor, a knight's effectiveness was only as good as his training. Wielding weapons from a saddle on a galloping horse was entirely different from fighting with a sword on the ground. A knight's years of

Early chain mail allowed freedom of movement but was easily penetrated by arrows, forcing the development of solid plate armor.

apprenticeship as a page and a squire properly prepared him for the challenge of being a great knight.

Battles and Tournaments

Since war was common in medieval Europe, there was no shortage of battles in which knights were needed. Hopkins describes them as ranging from "local conflicts between competing lords or cities, to national conflicts within Europe, such as the Hundred Years War."[3] So, knights had to be familiar with different types of military campaigns.

The most common military campaign was the raid. During a raid, a group of knights would take an enemy camp by surprise, hoping to cause great destruction while encountering no opposition. Raids were faster than and preferable to besieging a castle with the enemy safely ensconced behind its walls. A castle siege could involve a series of tactics. First, the invaders would try to starve the enemy by sealing them in, forcing them to deplete the limited food supply within the castle. There were three basic ways to penetrate the castle: The knights could climb the walls (which put them in the vulnerable position of being fired upon), weaken the walls by pummeling them or undermining them so that they would crumble, or try to break the gate down. Many different assault weapons were used to gain entry into the castle, including ballistas (giant crossbows), mangonels (giant catapults), and trebuchets (another type of catapult). They could also get inside by some sort of trickery. Whatever path the knights took, besieging a castle could be a time-consuming endeavor. The longer it took to get inside, the more challenges the warriors could incur outside the castle walls. Illness could befall them, or their own food supply could run out.

Although raids and sieges were more common than full-scale battles, knights were of paramount importance on the battlefield. Forming a line, lances out, they led the cavalry charge toward the enemy, mowing down as many as possible. After the initial engagement, the knights resorted to their other weapons and fought with all of the force with which they had been trained.

Even though most knights performed these military services out of loyalty in exchange for their fiefs (theoretically, their main source of livelihood), fiefs often did not provide enough. For that reason, the spoils of war were an added bonus to any knight's participation. A knight could take anything from a defeated enemy, from food to livestock to weapons to horses. He could also take an enemy knight or noble as his hostage and hold him until a ransom was paid. While other ranks of enemy forces were often killed, knights were spared because of their ransom value.

On the trail of battle, a knight's life was harsh. Even if he survived a skirmish, he could die from disease, starvation, or even a festering wound. Richard the Lionheart died of gangrene (an infection) caused by an arrow wound in his shoulder. Medical treatment was extremely limited during this period of history. Aware of the fragility of good health, besiegers often catapulted "stinking carcasses of horses or sheep over [enemy] walls in the hope of spreading disease among the people,"[4] says Hopkins.

The pursuit of honor was essential to the knight's identity and was his motivation for participating and succeeding in battle. The more he succeeded, the more honor he attained. Cowardice and dishonor were unacceptable to a knight. He had trained for years, and he risked his life every time he engaged an enemy.

Historian Richard Barber notes that the knight "acquired his skill in arms in two ways: in real warfare, and in practice in arms off the battlefield."[5] In the tenth century, knights began practicing without any central supervision, in a format that later developed into the tournament. Tournaments were mock wars in which the goal was to capture a competitor instead of killing him. However,

German knights joust at a tournament. These competitions were not only sporting events but also training grounds for the knights of Europe.

early tournaments were bloody and even fatal. Knights divided into two small armies and then charged each other. Inevitably, men were killed or badly hurt. For a peacetime gathering that was meant to give knights an opportunity to display their skills, the tournament became heavily criticized for its violence. In fact, tournaments occasionally sparked feuds, and the church, as well as King Henry II, banned them in the twelfth century. After Henry II died, tournaments resumed, and by 1316, the pope decided to withdraw the church's ban because tournaments served as a training arena for knights needed for the Crusades.

However, the tournaments became better organized, with rules and individual contests such as the joust. According to Hopkins,

> Rule books were drawn up for tournaments, such as Edward I's, which insisted on the use of blunted . . . weapons, restricted the number of men who could accompany a knight, and ordained that foot soldiers and grooms should not be armed. . . . Knights . . . had to register and, in some places, to pay a fee.[6]

Young knights benefited from tournaments. They were another forum in which to improve their skills and build a reputation. Some older knights made a living out of winning at tournaments;

the prizes were usually an opponent's horse and armor. Tournaments became celebrated events.

The Church's Role

The Norman conquest of Anglo-Saxon England resulted in the strong presence of the church. Death was all too prevalent in medieval society, and the church filled a void, furnishing everyone from kings to peasants with hope. An astonishing number of abbeys and cathedrals were built during this period, which is, in and of itself, a testament to the medieval reverence for religion. It could take a hundred years to build one cathedral. "No one could walk far without coming across a church, monastery, friary or priory,"[7] says Hopkins. The church became involved in local government and education and had its own lands, donated by nobles. The church in turn became a landlord to knights, rendering it a powerful player in the feudal system.

The church helped to mold the knight's role into the chivalric ideal. Offering honor and redemption as rewards for appropriate violent behavior, such as the defense of the poor or of the church, helped to end guerrilla-type violence. By the twelfth century, the church took over the dubbing of new knights, replacing what had been a chieftain-type ceremony with a Christian one. The candidate prayed through the night, wore symbolic Christian colors, and ultimately pledged his loyalty to God.

The Crusades

In 1071, Seljuk Turks captured the holy city of Jerusalem, thereby denying access to Christians. The Christian response came in the form of the Crusades. In November 1095, Pope Urban II, who was the son of a French knight, appealed to all knights for help:

> God exhorts you as heralds of Christ . . . knights as well
> as foot-soldiers, rich and poor, to hasten to exterminate
> this vile race [the Seljuk Turks] from our lands and to aid
> the Christian inhabitants in time.[8]

He assured them that if they served God in this holy war, they would "attain an eternal reward."[9] For a knight who already was "a pious hero charged with protecting the persons and the property of the Church, as well as the weak, the poor, the widows, and the orphans—all in the name of God . . . his supreme task was now the struggle against the infidel," says historian Georges Tate.[10]

The first crusaders won back Jerusalem, but lost it again, prompting the Second Crusade in 1147. There were eight Crusades in all,

Warriors prepare to launch a catapult against a Turkish stronghold during the First Crusade.

spanning 134 years. Ultimately, as before the Crusades began, the Holy Land was left to Muslim control.

The Crusades contributed to the knight's purpose, offering him a life in the pursuit of eternity rather than remaining at home engaged in battle on behalf of someone else. For many knights who had no lands of their own from which to draw an income, or who had little success on the tournament circuit, being a crusader knight was a great opportunity.

Regardless of whether knights volunteered to defeat the "infidels" or to gain eternal life—in the hope of obtaining land or gold along the way—the church's appeal fell on enthusiastic ears. There was no lack of adventurous participants for the First Crusade, which, according to Tate, turned out to be "marked by carnage, pillage, and destruction: the massacre of Jews in the Rhineland; thieving and slaughter in Hungary and the Byzantine Empire."[11] The journey was long and difficult, plagued by illness and lack of food and water. Crusader knights, if they survived, led arduous lives.

CHAPTER 2

William Marshal, Loyalty Above All Else

William Marshal's life was a remarkable one. During his lifetime, which was long according to standards of his day, he accomplished more than most of his contemporaries. As a knight, he excelled above all others; in addition, he became an adviser to England's royal family, was appointed a baron, served as a regent for a boy king, and just before he died, became a Templar monk. What makes Marshal's story extraordinary is the fact that, as a landless fourth son of a minor baron, he had few, if any, prospects for success. In a feudal society such as England, rising beyond one's station was difficult and unlikely. Marshal's rise to fame and fortune resulted from his complete dedication to the knightly virtues of which he never lost sight: courage, wisdom, generosity, and, most of all, loyalty. Even Marshal's enemy, King Philip of France, would one day hail him as "the most loyal man and true I have ever known, in any country I have been."[12]

Beginnings

William Marshal was born around 1145 (his birth was so insignificant that it was not recorded, and historians now give a general period). He was the fourth son born to John Marshal, who was a marshal and captain to Empress Matilda.

The first major chronicled event of William's life occurred when he was approximately six years old. It was a time of civil war in England. King Henry I had died, and his daughter, Empress Matilda, married to Geoffrey Plantagenet, count of Anjou, was fighting her French cousin Stephen, count of Boulogne, to guard the throne for her infant son Henry. Stephen believed he was entitled to the throne because he was a male descendant of William the Conqueror and was old enough to rule. In the early stages of the conflict, John Marshal served Stephen, but he soon switched allegiances when he thought he could benefit more on Matilda's side.

John Marshal may have been brave, but he showed no more loyalty to his family than he did to his ruler. Stephen laid siege to John Marshal's castle and forced him to turn over his son William as a hostage to guarantee that John would honor a truce that had been struck, which was a common practice of the time. However, instead of honoring the truce, John proceeded to reinforce his garrison and told the king that he still had "the hammer and the forge to produce another such [son], even finer."[13] The king was entitled to kill William in retaliation, and his men urged him to catapult the boy over the castle walls. When William spied the giant catapult, he thought it was a swing on which to play. Stephen could not bring himself to kill such an innocent child for his father's defiance, and vowed that he would never harm William. Eventually, when the conflict was settled and Matilda had surrendered, Stephen returned William to his family unharmed. Stephen agreed to name Matilda's son Henry as his successor since he had no heirs of his own and wanted peace. Henry became king in 1154, and John Marshal was awarded the manors of Cherhill, Marlborough, and Wexcombe for his support of Matilda.

The wife of Stephen pleads with his rival cousin, Matilda, on behalf of her husband during their dispute over the throne.

Perhaps young William's experience as a hostage laid the seeds for him to grow into a self-sufficient adult, one who would always strive to be independent.

Knight-in-Training

Historians know little about the next seven years of William's life. What is certain is that under feudal law, as a fourth son, William was entitled to inherit nothing. One option open to sons with such limited prospects was to be trained for knighthood. In 1159, when William was thirteen, he went to train with Lord William de Tancarville, a cousin of John Marshal's.

At Lord Tancarville's castle for the next eight years, William learned how to care for armor and horses, how to hunt, and how to sing. He served as a table squire and trained for battle. William was also taught how to wrestle, to ride in full armor, and to use weapons such as the shortbow, ax, mace, and sword. He demonstrated a natural ability for such training. At the same time, William also earned a reputation for excessive drinking, sleeping, and eating. He ignored the criticism of his behavior, focusing on the day when he would be proclaimed a knight. That moment finally came when Lord Tancarville was ordered to help King Henry II fight King Louis VII of France by defending the Norman camp at Drincourt.

Now a young man of twenty-one, Marshal was a handsome, brown-haired squire. He had looked forward to being knighted, which was an elaborate ceremony by the twelfth century. Prior to this, a new knight was simply dubbed by placing the flat of a sword on his shoulders or head. By Marshal's time, however, the ceremony had become a Christian one. On the eve of knighthood, the candidate bathed, symbolically washing away his sins. Then he was clothed in a white tunic or robe, symbolizing his purity. He would keep vigil through the night in an abbey, kneeling at the altar with his sword, dedicating his life to God, his king, and his lord. In the morning he would receive his armor, spurs, and sword and be dubbed by a knight or royal figure. Celebration would follow. But England was at war and there was no time for such traditions. Tancarville gave Marshal a new cloak, a horse, belt, and sword, quickly dubbed him a knight, and then sent him off to battle.

Marshal proved his worth the next day, fighting savagely. Medievalist Sidney Painter says that Marshal demonstrated incredible stamina and strength when "a Flemish serjeant caught him by the shoulder with an iron hook. Although he was dragged from his horse in the midst of hostile foot-soldiers, he managed to disengage the hook and cut his way out."[14] Even though his horse was killed, Marshal was proud and seemed invincible. While Marshal was primed for more fighting, France and England declared peace. Tancarville was forced to reduce his household. Without any prospects, Marshal sold his knight's cloak to buy a horse to carry his armor. Fortunately, Tancarville recruited Marshal to participate in a tournament under his banner that autumn. This marked the beginning of tournament winnings for Marshal, who quickly earned a reputation for being the strongest and bravest knight.

The next year, on a winter break from tournaments, Marshal asked to join the military household of his mother's brother, Earl Patrick of Salisbury. Patrick was thrilled to have his skilled nephew join him as he was preparing to go to Poitou, France, to help Henry II put down rebels who were destroying his properties. One day, while Patrick and Marshal were escorting King Henry II's wife, Eleanor of Aquitaine, to a safe castle in Lusignan, France, they were attacked. The castle had only recently been seized for Henry, and a force led by the castle's previous owners approached. While the queen fled safely, Marshal and his uncle engaged the enemy in battle. Even though Marshal's uncle was unarmed, the attackers stabbed him to death. Marshal was enraged and rushed into the enemy, fighting wildly. With sixty-eight men against him, Marshal was wounded and taken prisoner. He could have turned and galloped off once he realized that he was outnumbered, but out of loyalty to his uncle, Marshal stayed and fought. Such bravery caught the attention of the queen. After her safe return, Eleanor traded hostages for Marshal's release and awarded him money, horses, and arms. She thought he was the best knight in the land. Perhaps more important to Marshal's future, he was also appointed as the military tutor to the king and queen's son, fifteen-year-old Prince Henry.

Royal Tutor

Marshal embarked on what proved to be a lucrative career. He was twenty-two years old, and while many men of his era would have married and started a family, Marshal owned no lands that would provide income with which to support a family. But since he was a remarkably able knight, he continued to enter tournaments whenever he could, and won great purses. He was also in the privileged position of tutoring the prince on knightly virtues, how to use weapons, and how to fight in battles and tournaments. Sometimes Prince Henry went with Marshal to tournaments, and the two became close friends. The prince's coronation was held in 1170 when he was eighteen.

As well as Marshal's life was going, signs of trouble were clear. Prince Henry may have been crowned the next king, but his father withheld what he wanted desperately, which was to rule. Henry II was not about to give up his throne. Giving away titles, lands, and money to his sons was an attempt to appease them with something while retaining the throne for himself.

In 1173, the Young King, now twenty-one, decided to lead a revolt against his father, with his brothers and the king of France as allies. Young Henry had one problem, though: He was not yet knighted. Although bestowing knighthood was usually reserved for royalty to perform, the Young King asked Marshal to perform the ceremony. According to Painter, "to receive his king into the order of chivalry was a signal honor for a landless knight. Nothing could demonstrate more clearly the high place William had gained in his master's esteem."[15]

King Henry II (pictured) was drawn into a bloody rebellion after ignoring his son's claim to the throne.

The rebellion lasted a year and a half, during which time many of the Young King's knights abandoned him for the king. But Marshal did not. Historians agree that he probably identified with the Young King's problems with his father because of the way Marshal had been treated by his own father. Eventually, Henry II signed treaties with all of his sons as well as with the French king. Since Marshal had remained loyal to the Young King throughout the rebellion, his position in the king's eyes could have been considered treasonous. However, the king did not condemn Marshal; in fact, the knight emerged from the rebellion in a stronger position than ever because Henry II respected Marshal for his loyalty to his son.

In 1182, when Marshal was thirty-seven and the young king thirty, rumors began that Marshal was having an affair with the Young King's wife, Marguerite. Marshal's close relationship with his lord had fueled jealousy among the household. Although Marshal staunchly denied the accusation, Young Henry reluctantly believed it. Punishment for such treason was banishment. Marshal left the court but returned at Christmas, insisting he be able to fight his accusers. He offered to have a finger cut off his right hand before combat, and should he be defeated, the Young King could have him hanged. But no one would fight him. Sadly, Marshal was banished. Soon, however, renewed conflict arose between Henry II and the Young King, and Marshal was summoned to help young Henry, the alleged adultery forgotten.

The Young King was destined never to rule England, as he fell ill with dysentery and died at the age of thirty-one. On his deathbed, the prince asked Marshal to take his cloak with the crusader's cross to the Holy Sepulcher in Jerusalem. (Every knight carried such a cross, and to prove his devotion to God, each was supposed to bring it to the site of Jesus' tomb.) The Young King left behind considerable financial debts, which out of loyalty Marshal initially set out to pay. Marshal also reported to King Henry that his son had asked for the king's forgiveness. Henry II was deeply saddened at the loss of his son.

Henry II was eager to have his late son's loyal servant join his household, but before Marshal would do so, he proceeded to fulfill the Young King's request and set off on the long, hot, two-year journey to Jerusalem. By making this journey, Marshal demonstrated his devotion to the Young King as well as to knighthood.

Landowner

Upon Marshal's return from the Holy Land in 1187 (at the age of forty-two), Henry II awarded him with the royal position of *familiaris regis* (wise counselor). Marshal was also to serve Henry II as the captain of his knights. But more important to Marshal's future security was Henry's gift of a fief, a large piece of land, along with the services of all the peasants who lived on the land. For the first time in his life, Marshal had a guaranteed annual income. Since his tournament days were over, Marshal embarked in military service for his king, fighting the French in one battle after another. Eventually, Henry's next son in line for the throne, Richard, would join the French forces against him. With his sons abandoning him, Henry II appreciated Marshal's loyalty and counsel all

Marshal demonstrated his loyalty to King Henry's son by fulfilling his dying request to journey to the Holy Sepulchre in Jerusalem.

the more. He rewarded him with the promise of the second richest heiress in England, Isabel de Clare of Striguil, for his wife. Such promises were, at the time, the king's to make. Under feudal law, the king could appropriate daughters and widows of wealthy barons and then award them as brides to whomever he chose. It turned out to be Henry's son Richard who actually bestowed the seventeen-year-old heiress upon Marshal, for Henry died before he could do so. Having been weakened by years of warfare, Henry II died in 1189 at the age of fifty-six.

Once again, Marshal was left in a precarious position, this time because of his allegiance to Henry. Yet, again, Marshal's loyalty served him as Richard recognized that Marshal had performed his duty as a knight with perfect devotion to his liege lord. Furthermore, Richard wanted Marshal's services and the same kind of loyalty. He appointed Marshal as one of four justiciars (assistants) to the chancellor, William Longchamp.

Honoring his father's promise, Richard bestowed Isabel upon Marshal. Her holdings included the castles of Striguil and Orbec, the Goodrich fortress, half the barony of Longueville, two manors, the service of forty-three knights, and one-quarter of Ireland. Now William Marshal, at forty-four years old, was lord of Striguil, of Longueville, and of Leinster. Marshal and his wife settled into a thirty-year marriage. Over the next ten years, they had ten children.

Royal Service

Marshal's position was all the more significant because King Richard dedicated his ten-year reign to the Crusades. As a result, he was rarely in England. Running the country largely fell to Longchamp and Marshal. Richard's absence tempted his younger brother, John, to try to take the throne. Once again, William Marshal found himself in between warring royal family members. This time, his position was even more complex because Marshal's Irish lands were ultimately under John's domain, but he was personally pledged to Richard's service. Painter explains:

> Richard was king of England, and to him was due the primary allegiance of the barons of the realm. On the other hand, John was lord of Ireland by the gift of Henry II, and William had done him homage for Leinster. If Richard himself tried to invade Ireland, William would be bound to aid John.[16]

Marshal demonstrated loyalty throughout his life, and these circumstances were no different. Marshal refused to pay the king homage for his Irish lands, yet he stood beside him in Richard's war against John. According to Painter, "In England William served Richard, in Ireland John. He was not only scrupulous in his interpretation of his feudal obligations, but also courageous in performing them."[17]

Marshal's dilemma resolved itself after Richard died from complications of an arrow wound in his shoulder in 1199. Richard had no children of his own, so the question was whether the

King John proved an inept and wasteful ruler and his nobles finally forced him to sign the Magna Carta in 1215.

throne belonged to John or to Arthur, John's twelve-year-old nephew. Marshal played a key role in influencing the archbishop of Canterbury to choose John. Although Marshal was not particularly fond of John, he believed that as the fourth son of Henry II, he was more entitled to the throne than Henry's grandson was. John showed his gratitude by designating the fifty-four-year-old Marshal as the earl of Pembroke and appointing him sheriff of Gloucestershire. Marshal had become a court favorite.

But all did not remain well between King John and Marshal. Constantly at war with France, King John decided to abandon Normandy. Since Marshal owned lands in Normandy, he was obliged to swear homage to King Philip, which also meant he could not take up arms against him. This angered John. Later, when King John asked Marshal to engage in battle against the French, he had to refuse. The king considered this unacceptable. As punishment, he demanded two of Marshal's sons as hostages for having such divided loyalties. Marshal, now advanced in age but still faithful to feudal law, handed over two sons and retired to Ireland, being out of royal favor.

From his refuge in Ireland, Marshal watched as John floundered as king of England. History shows that John lost most of England's holdings in France, quarreled with the nobles, and bled the royal coffers dry, hopelessly funding failed military expeditions. He had resorted to raiding nobles' properties and burning them to the ground if they would not join him. Eventually, the nobles forced the king to sign the Magna Carta in 1215, a document limiting the king's power and giving more power to the barons, thereby founding England's parliamentary government. A year after signing the document, in October 1216, King John died from dysentery, without any friends or noble support. But to Marshal's surprise, he learned that John had asked for Marshal's forgiveness and that his young nine-year-old son, Henry, be placed in Marshal's care.

Regent

Ten days after King John's death, his son was crowned King Henry III. However, he could not rule until he reached maturity. Because of Marshal's experience with the royal family, his success as a knight and warrior, his infinite wisdom, honesty, and loyalty, the nobles asked him to rule in the meantime, under the title "regent of England." Although he was reluctant to assume such a huge responsibility in his old age, Marshal saw a boy who could be abandoned if he did not step in, an image with which he could identify. He accepted the job.

With no money in the treasury to finance a defense against a pressing French invasion into England, Marshal immediately implemented an intelligent strategy. He sold all of the royal jewels and valuables to retain John's unpaid army who had been itching to desert the Crown and find their fortunes elsewhere. In the name of their new Young King, Henry III, they marched to Dover. In his prebattle address, Marshal inspired his knights:

> To protect our valor, for us, for those who love us, for our wives and our children, for the defense of our lands, in order to win the highest honor, for the peace of the Church as well, for the remission of our sins, let us bear the weight of arms. . . . You are the hope of the country. . . . Behold, those men are in your hand. They are ours, if your hearts serve you boldly now, without fail. If we die, God will take us to His paradise. If we defeat them, we shall have acquired lasting honor for ourselves and our descendants.[18]

The English forces defeated the French, blocking and capturing the French fleet in the English Channel. Though Marshal could have taken Prince Louis captive, he instead escorted him to the coast, perhaps showing leniency toward the French for the sake of his personal lands in France. Later, back at home, Marshal met with the nobles to assure them of their importance to the new king and the trust he placed in them. This was especially important because many of them had been ready to rebel against King John alongside

Prince Louis. With a long-sought peace, a recovering treasury, and the support of the nobles, Marshal's term as regent was highly successful and stabilizing to a ravaged and financially strained England.

Death

Three years after becoming regent, Marshal, now seventy-four years old, was struck with an unnamed, sudden illness in January 1219. He deteriorated quickly, dying three months later. On his deathbed, he issued orders that would take care of everyone he loved. Yet he showed that even loyalty must serve integrity. As historian Georges Duby writes, Marshal lectured the Young King and "pray[ed] God . . . to bring him to immediate ruin should he become, by some mischance, a traitor in the unfortunate fashion of some of his forebears."[19]

William Marshal exhibited unwavering loyalty and strictly followed the feudal code of honor over the course of his long life.

To his four older sons, William Marshal left lands and estates. His oldest son, also named William, would naturally inherit the major family lands after his mother, Countess Isabel, had died. His youngest son, Anselm, like himself so long ago, was owed nothing, but Marshal broke with feudal tradition, leaving him some land in Ireland worth 140 pounds per year. Four of Marshal's five daughters were already married to nobles. To the last, Jeanne, still unmarried, he left a dowry (land worth thirty pounds a year and two hundred marks in cash) to attract a husband. Continuing his adherence to the knightly virtues of generosity and protecting the weak, Marshal also left instructions that, upon his death, one hundred peasants be clothed and fed. Marshal desired the people to pray for his soul, and feeding and clothing them was a small gift to them for doing so.

He bequeathed various sums of money to different abbeys as well. Also, on his deathbed, Marshal revealed to his family that, while in Jerusalem, he had committed himself to becoming a member of the military religious order of Knights Templar. The time had now come. As he lay dying, Marshal gave his wife a final kiss and was then covered with a white cloak embellished with the red cross. Brother Aimery de Sainte-Maure, the master of the temple, arrived and accepted Marshal into the Templar Order, guaranteeing him life after death with God. According to Painter, with this act, "the identification of the virtues pleasing to God with the chivalric ones of prowess, wisdom, and loyalty is complete."[20] Marshal had sent a friend for two silken cloths that he had brought back from the Holy Land thirty years before, and he instructed that they be put over his body upon burial.

Upon his death, Marshal's body rested in state overnight while retinues of nobles filed past it. He was given a funeral procession with a guard of honor and a mass at Westminster Abbey performed by the archbishop of Canterbury; then, he was buried in the Temple Church. Marshal's funeral was grander than those of the kings he had served, with the exception of Richard I.

To preserve his father's renowned life, Marshal's eldest son hired a poet to compose a poem to celebrate it. After seven years of compiling the material and writing and editing, the poem had grown to 19,914 verses. It is considered to be one of the first pieces of French literature, and it is the earliest French biography to have been preserved through the ages. The poet's surname is unknown; he is referred to only as Jean "le Trouvere," the French noun for "finder," hence the man who found the information to write the poem.

Marshal died highly revered by those who knew him and knew of him. He was an exemplary knight, nobleman, and diplomat and served four kings. In his unrelenting dedication to the knightly virtues—honor, courage, fidelity to one's word, generosity, prowess in battle, and especially loyalty—William Marshal had been a shining example to all. One of his contemporaries, Jean de Rouvray, was heard to praise Marshal upon his death: "I judge that this was the wisest knight that was ever seen, in any land, in our age."[21]

CHAPTER 3

Richard the Lionheart, Crusader King

Richard I was the king of England from 1189 to 1199. He spent half of his reign defending his French lands and the other half preparing for and leading the Third Crusade. The fact that he spent only six months of his reign physically in England and could not speak English has led to criticism that he was a poor English king. However, a warrior first, Richard I proved his bravery time and again, personally leading his men into many battles and always confident of his ability to win the day. In fact, he was called Richard Lionheart (from the French, *Coeur de Leon*) because he was a brave and fearless warrior. It was even rumored that he fought a lion bare-handed. The picture of a lion became the symbol on his flag and armor. The war against the infidel was the ultimate fight for a knight of his time, and historically Richard is considered the bravest crusader there was, epitomizing the code of chivalry.

Childhood

Richard was born on September 8, 1157, at Beaumont Palace in Oxford, England, to Henry II, the first Angevin king of England, and Eleanor of Aquitaine, two of the most renowned figures of medieval history. When Henry became king in 1154, bringing to the throne his mother's French lands of Anjou and Eleanor's French duchy of Aquitaine (the western half of France), he became the most powerful regent in Europe. To rule effectively, Henry II traveled around his kingdom extensively. He was an outdoorsman who lived for the hunt, and he did not miss the majesty and ceremony of court. Eleanor was the opposite, beautiful, vibrant, and the life of the court. Twelve years his senior, she had previously been married to King Louis VII of France, but after fourteen years of marriage she had not borne a son, and Louis had the marriage annulled. After marrying Henry, Eleanor gave birth to five children in six years; they would have eight all together. The first born, William, died in his infancy. The second child was a girl, and the third, Henry, would be raised as heir to his father's throne. Richard, the fourth child, Eleanor decided, would be heir to her lands of Aquitaine.

As was normal for royals, baby Richard was passed to a wet nurse, named Hodierna, for suckling. It is unknown how much time Richard spent in Hodierna's care, but historian Geoffrey Regan points out that "in the first year of Richard's life . . . it has been estimated that [his parents] traveled over 3,500 miles, on horseback."[22] During Richard's early childhood, his father was rarely at home, and historian John Gillingham suggests that "it was inevitable that for Richard and his brothers and sisters their father was a distant figure, always in a hurry."[23]

Eleanor of Aquitaine was the powerful wife of Henry II of England. Her son Richard would become a famous crusader king.

The true importance of royal children lay in the potential marriage alliances they might bring. Richard was betrothed at the age of two to the daughter of Raymond Berengar IV, the count of Barcelona. So, Richard (and his brothers and sisters) was not expected to look forward to a loving marriage.

In 1165, when Richard was eight years old, Eleanor decided to take him and his sister Matilda to Normandy. There is very little chronicled about Richard's childhood, but most historians assume that he learned the skills typical of twelfth-century royal sons. In addition to knightly skills (at which he excelled), Richard would have been educated in Latin. Indeed, as an adult he spoke Latin exceptionally well, and could write verse in French. He was never taught the English language, however, having spent most of his youth in France. "What may have marked Richard out from his fellows," says Regan, "was his poetic and musical ability, which was cultivated to a high level at the court of Eleanor of Aquitaine."[24] The fact that Richard spent more time in his mother's presence than the king's is indisputable. Their last child, John, was born in 1167 when Richard was ten. By 1170, Henry and Eleanor were unofficially separated.

Richard remained at his mother's court in Poitou, France, while his brothers Henry, Geoffrey, and John stayed with Henry II. Being brought up in a divided household set the stage for Richard to eventually rebel against his father. At Eleanor's court, Richard was exposed to troubadours, intellectuals, and tournaments, and he inherited her dedication to the Crusades. In the days of her marriage to King Louis, the two had taken up the cross and inspired the Second Crusade. Although it failed, the idea of conquest over the infidels must have remained dear to her heart. Eventually, Richard would take up the cause and become the famous crusader king.

Duke of Aquitaine

In June 1172, at the age of fourteen, Richard was installed as the duke of Aquitaine. Eleanor made it a grand celebration. The teenage duke was now responsible for the defense of Aquitaine, and because of the troubles brewing between his older brother Henry (crowned the Young King two years earlier), and their father, Richard was to assume even more responsibility as part of a rebellion.

The Young King, although crowned, had not been given any lands over which to rule by Henry II, and he had become increasingly agitated over it. Now, Richard had Aquitaine and Geoffrey had Brittany. After the family spent a tense Christmas together, during which Henry II blamed Eleanor for encouraging rebelliousness in their sons, the Young King rallied Richard and Geoffrey with him to Louis VII's court to take up arms against their father.

Richard's position as duke of Aquitaine meant that he already gave allegiance to Louis VII, and having his own lands may have contributed to the division between him and his father. In the spring of 1173, Richard and his brothers swore not to make peace with Henry II without Louis VII's consent. Significantly, it was Louis VII who knighted Richard. He was fifteen years old. Gillingham makes the following analysis of the family rebellion:

Henry II would need to have been an unusually stupid man not to realize that there were bound to be difficult moments in the relationship between him and his heir. But he is unlikely to have foreseen . . . that Eleanor and his other sons were also plotting against him. . . . Presumably he believed that . . . she would not want to carry her opposition to the point of war—particularly if that were to involve her in an alliance with her ex-husband. . . . It was an astonishing decision. That a Queen should rebel against the King her husband was something so unbelievable.[25]

Despite the brotherly alliance with Louis VII, Henry II's forces proved to be stronger. He made his way through Aquitaine looking for Eleanor. Hearing of his approach, the queen fled, disguised as a knight, but was nonetheless captured. Henry imprisoned her, and she would remain imprisoned for the duration of his reign. Now sixteen years old, Richard was devastated by his mother's fate. Until this point in the rebellion, he had remained in the background of an argument that was mainly between his father and the Young King. Now he was deeply angry with his father for the treatment of his mother and he took charge of the rebellion in Poitou.

Richard would not win against Henry II at this time, however. Deserted by the Young King and Louis VII, who had already agreed to a truce with Henry, Richard was forced to retreat, until finally he surrendered. "On 23 September [1174]," writes Gilligham, "he entered his father's presence. Weeping, he threw himself flat on his face at Henry's feet and begged forgiveness."[26] Henry II did so, offering the kiss of peace, but he reduced Richard's holdings in Aquitaine and would not release Eleanor.

Over the next nine years, between 1174 and 1183, Richard looked after Aquitaine. It was not a simple task, as Richard had to quell one uprising after another of French nobles attempting to rid themselves of Henry II's rule. These years proved to be the learning ground that shaped Richard's military strategy and contributed to the leadership skills that would serve him tremendously during the Third Crusade. Richard became a specialist at besieging castles, attacking those that others would never consider. He even captured the coveted Taillebourg, thought to be an impregnable fortress. It was protected by a sheer rock face on three sides and had a well-fortified fourth side. It took Richard three days to capture it. And while other leaders often sought the safety of the sidelines of a battle, Richard preferred to lead his men, charging alongside them, involved in the skirmishes first-hand. History has sometimes criticized Richard for this hands-on warrior approach because, as a leader, he had a responsibility to look after himself. Especially when he became king, his safety was of paramount importance to England. But that was never his style. As a knight, Richard's bravery and prowess in battle was unmatched.

Rebel

Family relations eventually became an issue once again, prompted by the Young King. During Christmas 1182, Henry II and all of

Richard I often led his troops into battle, preferring action to the safety of the sidelines.

his sons gathered at his court. The Young King wanted his brothers to pay him homage, but Richard refused. He felt that he was just as noble as his brother. Henry convinced Richard to reconsider, but when he did, the Young King rejected him and announced that he would take up arms against Richard. The bone of contention seemed to be the castle of Clairvaux, which Richard had fortified but which was on the Young King's lands. Even though Henry managed to get Richard to surrender Clairvaux to his brother, the tension mounted, and soon the two brothers were at war.

Chaos reigned in Aquitaine as barons who disliked Richard's rule joined the Young King's forces. But while the Young King attempted to be a leader, Richard outshone him in commitment and brutality. Regan says that Richard "drowned some of his captives, blinded others, and cut the throats of the remainder."[27] Seeing his empire crumbling, Henry II joined Richard against the Young King to try to put an end to it all. But it was the Young King's unexpected death from dysentery in June 1183 that ended it instead. Richard was now twenty-five and next in line for the throne.

Henry II ordered Richard to give Aquitaine to his younger brother John, presumably because Richard would one day be king. Richard refused to give it up, and finally Henry told John to invade it. Richard readied his forces and fought back. Cunningly, Henry, using Richard's love for his mother against him, temporarily released Eleanor, asking Richard to surrender Aquitaine to her. Richard was thrilled to see his mother restored to her duchy and laid down his arms.

During these years of family brawls, another king was observing the Angevin empire with great interest. Louis VII had died, leaving the French throne to his son, Philip II, who wanted nothing more than to break up what Henry II had built. Since his father had already been involved in providing a haven for Henry's unhappy offspring from time to time, Philip decided to attempt the same thing. Feigning friendship, he asked Richard to consider a Crusade with him.

Henry's relationship with the French king was constantly strained, and it was always over lands. But then, Philip's sister Alice became part of the equation. Richard's childhood betrothal had long since been replaced with a betrothal to Alice. However, Henry had delayed the marriage for years but held her in his court. Henry feared that, through Alice, Philip might try to claim back what were once French lands but now part of Henry's

Angevin empire. Richard believed that his father had seduced Alice and wanted nothing to do with her.

As the quarrel over Alice's fate escalated between Henry and Philip, enthusiasm for a Crusade was everywhere. Under a new leader, Saladin, Muslims had annihilated the army of Jerusalem in July 1187. The general populace talked about it and troubadours sang about it. That autumn, Richard took the cross to a cathedral and became the first prince to publicly claim his intention to go on a Crusade. He did not ask Henry's permission, demonstrating an independence from his father once and for all. Richard began working with Philip II on a joint Crusade, leaving Henry II out of the loop, which naturally caused Henry great worry. After a year of tension, the three men met. For hostility to cease, Philip's condition was simply that Alice be married to Richard. Henry refused. Then Richard asked his father to recognize him as his heir and Henry did not answer. "Now at last," said Richard, "I must believe what I had always thought was impossible."[28] Richard thereby came to believe that his father might be holding the throne for his younger brother John. Richard turned to Philip and swore homage to him. The relationship between Henry II and thirty-one-year-old Richard was over.

Richard and Philip launched a campaign against Henry and easily beat him back in a few short months. Henry II was weakened by illness and surrendered, hissing in Richard's ear, "God grant that I may not die until I have had a fitting revenge on you."[29] He died three days later, on July 6, 1189. Richard was now king of England.

Coronation

On September 3, 1189, Richard was crowned king. He was anointed with holy water by the archbishop of Canterbury in Westminster Abbey in a spiritual ceremony symbolizing the divine sanction of his kingship. Richard took three oaths, "guaranteeing to maintain the decrees of the Church, justice for his subjects and good laws and customs for the kingdom."[30] After the coronation, there was a mass. The three-day feast that followed involved 5,000 dishes, 1,720 pitchers, and 900 cups—a splendid testament to the pageantry that Richard and his mother loved.

The first order of business was to raise funds for a Crusade, which Richard I went about methodically and effectively. He sold everything he could, such as castles, but he also sold rights

The seaside city of Acre surrenders to the Crusaders. Richard joined forces with King Philip II of France to defeat the Muslims of Acre.

to holding public offices, titles, and privileges. Richard announced, "I would sell London if I could find a buyer."[31] Ships were commandeered and stocked with supplies; Richard planned to undertake the first sea-borne Crusade. In consideration of the threat that his two brothers posed during Richard's absence, he ordered that Geoffrey be ordained a priest. To John, he gave lands to call his own with the hope that he would be content and not try to take his throne. He appointed trusted and loyal men, as well as Eleanor, to run the wheels of government, and on December 12, 1189, three months after his coronation, Richard I sailed from Dover.

Crusader King

Besides the obvious appeal to a warrior like Richard of conquering the infidel, launching a Crusade offered the ultimate reward, eternal life. Clearly, Richard I was a religious man. When a hermit rebuked him for his sins, he ignored him at first. But after he became ill, he "did penance" for his sins and "tried to lead a better life,"[32] according to Roger of Howden, a chronicler who accompanied the Crusade. For Richard, there could be no greater glory than to take back the Holy Land. He was a knight, a leader of knights, and a seasoned warrior with more money and supplies than any previous crusaders. It was the popular struggle of his times, and he wanted to lead the Christians to victory.

Aware of Philip II's interest in the Angevin empire, Richard delayed departure from France to "Outremer" (land beyond the sea) until Philip was ready also. Even though the Crusade united the two leaders, neither could fully trust the other because of old quarrels. They both swore to protect all crusaders and defend each other's lands. On July 4, 1190, Richard I's and Philip II's armies embarked from Marseilles, France, on their journey to the Holy Land. Along the way, Richard proved himself to be a resourceful and strategic leader, dealing with unexpected obstacles, but it would take them ten months to reach the Holy Land, a sea voyage that normally took fifteen days.

During the trip, Richard finally addressed the Alice question when he married another woman, Berengaria of Navarre. This union created a useful alliance for Richard with King Sancho VI of Navarre, a minor Spanish king whose lands bordered Richard's southern frontier. Eleanor seems to have negotiated the marriage; she was probably eager for her unmarried son to produce an heir as soon as possible. Unfortunately, the marriage would produce no children, and Richard and Berengaria would spend very little time together.

Richard and Philip's first military target was Acre, a seaside city taken by Saladin. Using the siege experience he had gained in Aquitaine, Richard built a movable siege tower, an impressive and expensive machine, and set his army to work on Acre's walls. During the siege, both Richard and Philip were stricken with scurvy and became very ill, losing their hair and nails. But true to the warrior within him, Richard continued to watch the action from a litter carried to the front lines. It took Richard and his army about two months to crumble enough walls to gain entry. Acre fell on July 12, 1191. With the capture of Acre, Philip decided to return home, despite Richard's protests. Philip promised not to invade Richard's lands, but Richard did not trust him.

Richard soon returned his attention to Acre and negotiating the terms of surrender with Saladin. Richard had three thousand Muslim prisoners with which to bargain a hefty ransom, and Saladin agreed to pay 200,000 dinars. However, Saladin exceeded the payment deadline, effectively delaying Richard's departure to conquer another city. As a result, Richard ordered the massacre of all of the prisoners. Richard has been heavily criticized for this act, being called barbaric and cruel. However, at the time, people viewed infidels as unimportant and believed that a Christian, in fact, glorified Christ by killing a pagan. And strategically, Richard could not afford to leave behind soldiers to guard these prisoners while he launched sieges in other cities. He was two thousand miles away from home in the midst of an amphibious operation. He made a tactical decision.

Richard's next goal was to take Jaffa, another coastal city, about a two weeks' march south of Acre. Taking coastal cities before marching inland to Jerusalem allowed Richard to access provisions from his fleet of ships as well as provide cover for his right flank. As the king approached Arsuf, Saladin's troops of Turkish archers attacked. Richard's army charged and bore down on the Turks with unrelenting force, winning the day. Richard I's soldiers praised his fierceness and bravery in battle. Three days later, they effortlessly captured Jaffa and decided to rest there a while.

Malek Saladin (pictured) was the sultan of Egypt and Syria, with whom Richard negotiated the surrender of Acre.

Now Richard had to decide whether to go on to conquer Jerusalem. Strategically, he knew it would be difficult to take, as well as to defend once taken, and he knew the city would truly never be secure if the Muslims persevered. He opened negotiations with Saladin. Richard argued,

> The Muslims and Franks are bleeding to death, the country is utterly ruined, and goods and lives have been sacrificed on both sides. . . . The time has come to stop this. . . . Jerusalem is for us an object of worship that we could not give up even if there were only one of us left. . . . To you the Cross is simply a piece of wood with no value. But for us it is of enormous importance. If the Sultan will deign to return it to us, we shall be able to make peace.[33]

Saladin maintained that Jerusalem was much more precious to his people because it was the place from which the prophet ascended to heaven, and the land had always been theirs.

The need for a settlement escalated when Richard received word that his brother John and Philip II had joined forces back home. It is reported that Richard rode to the top of a hill within sight of Jerusalem, "flung up his shield to cover his eyes, and, weeping, begged God that he might not have to look upon the city if he could not deliver it."[34] On July 4, 1192, Richard I's army began to withdraw. A couple more skirmishes with Saladin occurred before Richard's final departure, and he once again rode into battle, mowing down the enemy without hesitation. Saladin and Richard resumed negotiations and agreed on a three-year truce. On October 9, 1192, Richard set sail for home. Not only had he failed to free Jerusalem; he might already have lost his kingdom at home.

Captive

En route home, an unexpected event occurred that would alter Richard's plans for the next thirteen months. He was captured by Duke Leopold V of Austria, who held a grudge against him for insulting him during the Crusade. Leopold and his emperor, Henry VI, knew they could demand an unprecedented ransom for such a prize. Eleanor and the justiciars in England raised 100,000 marks, and Richard I was released on February 4, 1194. Meanwhile, John and Philip II were ransacking the Angevin empire.

When Richard arrived home, he set about to retake the castles John had stolen. Richard was obviously the more powerful of the two brothers, and John soon asked for his brother's mercy. Duke Leopold was excommunicated and told to repay the ransom. As for Richard's French lands that Philip had invaded, much work awaited the king. He would spend the next five years reasserting his authority in France.

Death

Richard I risked his life in battle numerous times, but his death came by a crossbow bolt outside his tent as he was taking a stroll. Supervising a siege, he had exited his tent without armor and was struck in the left shoulder. Gillingham writes, "Calmly he returned

King Richard bids farewell to the Holy Land from the deck of his ship.

Eleven days after being wounded by a crossbow bolt, Richard I died of infection at the age of forty-two.

to his tent as though nothing had happened. Once inside he tried to pull out the bolt but succeeded only in breaking off the wooden shaft, leaving the iron barb . . . embedded in the flesh."[35]

Since Richard lacked the medical skill to treat an infection, the wound became gangrenous, and Richard sent for his mother. Knowing he was dying, he confessed his sins and received extreme unction. Richard recognized John as his heir, but generously gave away one-quarter of his treasure to the poor. Then he forgave the man who had wounded him. Eleven days after being wounded, on April 7, 1199, Richard I died at forty-two years of age. At his request, his brain and internal organs were buried in the Poitevin abbey of Charroux, his heart in Rouen, and the rest of his body in the abbey church of Fontevrault at his father's feet.

As a crusader, Richard I followed the path considered the most honorable by knights: to fight for the Cross. But it was his leadership of the Third Crusade that made him famous in his own day and historically came to define his kingship. Although Richard I was duke of Aquitaine longer than a crusader, his actions as a crusader took place on a world stage. Even though he did not take Jerusalem, he captured Acre, Arsuf, and Jaffa, and negotiated a truce with Saladin over Jerusalem, which was much more than his predecessors had achieved. In accomplishing this, Richard I demonstrated brilliant military strategy, administrative skill (recruiting funds and loyal subordinates), and personal bravery and prowess on the battlefield that was not only a testament to him but inspired loyalty and confidence in all who followed him. Muslim chronicler Ibn al-Athir said that "Richard's courage, shrewdness, energy, and patience made him the most remarkable ruler of his times."[36]

CHAPTER 4

Saladin, Military Warrior

Saladin was a twelfth-century sultan of Egypt and ruler of Syria who was a formidable opponent of the crusaders. Beyond his leadership role, he was also a warrior for the Muslim cause who was completely devoted to the unity of Islam. Although Western culture perceived him to be an infidel (that is, opposed to Christianity and therefore a natural enemy), it is said that he was actually knighted by a Christian. He certainly exhibited chivalric behavior more often than not. He was extremely religious, and the Islamic faith was the reason for his career as a warrior and a leader. Always very generous, Saladin died a poor man. He always acted with fairness and integrity, perhaps to a fault. He was a courageous warrior and one of the most successful Muslim leaders in history.

Childhood

Forty years before the birth of Saladin, in 1098, a significant event occurred in the Middle East that would mark the path of Saladin's life. The Europeans launched the first Crusade, conquering Jerusalem and establishing the Kingdom of Jerusalem. The Muslim world now had an intruder. Saladin would be born into that world and taught from the beginning that the Christians did not belong.

Saladin was born in 1138 in the town of Takrit near Baghdad (in modern-day Iraq) to Kurdish parents. His father, Najm al-din Ayyub, was the castellan (governor) of Takrit; he had been awarded this position by the Arab leader Zengi in return for his aid. Ayyub continued to flourish under Zengi's rule as commander of the city of Baalbek, and eventually became the governor of Damascus (in modern-day Syria). Ayyub's brother, Shirkuh, who was to have a huge influence on Saladin's life, became a deputy in Zengi's army.

Saladin grew up in Baalbek and Damascus and received an education befitting a gentleman. He loved to read and learned easily. He studied theology, the history of the Arab people, biographies, genealogies, law, and Arabic grammar and script, and he knew much of the Koran by heart. (Muslims consider the Koran as God's final message to humankind proclaimed by the angel Gabriel to Mohammed.) Saladin was small in build but became known in Damascus for his generosity, good manners, and piety, virtues that would characterize his entire life. He was taught how to hunt and to hawk, and he became a skilled horseman, capable of fighting with sword, lance, and bow and arrow.

Saladin's father, Ayyub, was an intelligent man, wise in worldly affairs, and an excellent administrator. Saladin's uncle Shirkuh was, by contrast, a charismatic and ambitious leader in the military and a good soldier. The brothers had risen in their respective positions because of their own abilities, not because of birthright. Saladin would follow their path to become a great military leader, but historian P.H. Newby points out that it was never an easy road:

> [Saladin] came from no princely family and was not one of the predominantly Turkish ruling class. They despised him as an upstart and were jealous of his success. . . . He was a Kurd whose family came originally from a highland village in Greater Armenia. . . . Even after he had established himself as a great fighter for Islam Saladin was often at odds with the ruler . . . of all Moslems, the Caliph in Baghdad, who thought him . . . an outsider.[37]

Saladin had much of his father's diplomacy and administrative skills, but he also gained the military knowledge of his uncle.

During Saladin's youth, Zengi began the holy war by taking Edessa back from the Franks in 1144. He perceived the crusader states (consisting of the Kingdom of Jerusalem, Tripoli, Antioch, and Edessa) as a threat to the Muslim world because their existence strategically blocked Syria from uniting with Egypt. Zengi wanted to unite Syria and Egypt under one ruler and one religion—Islam—in order to create a formidable force against the Christian Europeans. Part of the reason that the crusaders had gained ground in the Middle East so far was because not all Muslims were united. In retaliation, the Europeans launched the Second Crusade. Zengi did not live long enough to fight them, but his son, Nur al-Din (also spelled Nur ad-Din), succeeded him in 1146. Under his leadership, the crusaders were destroyed two years later just outside the walls of Damascus. Nur al-Din was a devout man and greatly influenced Saladin as he matured from a young boy to a soldier.

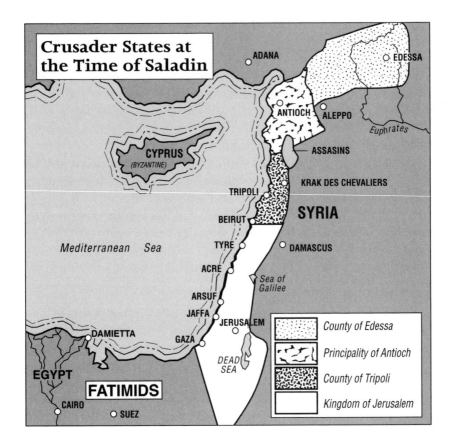

Crusader States at the Time of Saladin

Protégé

By his eighteenth birthday, Saladin had become a liaison officer for Nur al-Din. As the leader's protégé, Saladin rarely left his side. Nur al-Din's objective to unite Islam became Saladin's goal as well. In 1163, when Saladin was twenty-five, Nur al-Din decided to launch an invasion of Egypt, led by Shirkuh, and he ordered Saladin to accompany his uncle. The Egyptian rulers, called the Fatimid caliphate, practiced the Shiite form of Islam, dividing them from the Syrians' Sunni theology (the other branch of Islam). As Shirkuh's lieutenant, Saladin set out on what would be a series of campaigns between 1164 and 1168. During one of the expeditions in 1167, Saladin was given command of a Muslim center and successfully defeated a Frankish/Egyptian army. He was then entrusted with holding a fortified Syrian base at Alexandria, Egypt, with only a thousand men. He held it for three months, against besieger armies larger than his own, winning the esteem of Shirkuh and many emirs (Muslim rulers). Years later, Saladin said,

"What I went through in Alexandria I shall never forget,"[38] and he never wanted to set foot in Egypt again. It is said that, during the siege, Saladin was knighted by the leader of the Frankish army, but it was a Christian chronicler who claimed this. It seems unlikely that Saladin would agree to be a Christian knight. Regardless, Saladin's first leadership role had been successful.

Nur al-Din wanted to send Shirkuh and Saladin on yet another expedition, but after Alexandria, Saladin refused. He suspected that Shirkuh was planning to rule Egypt independently from Nur al-Din, and he did not wish to be dragged into such treachery. However, his father convinced him that it was his duty to go and be loyal to his uncle. Saladin said later, "I went as to my grave."[39] Shirkuh successfully overthrew the vizier (adviser) of Egypt and

Malek Saladin exhibited characteristic knightly chivalry, although Christian Europe viewed him as an infidel.

became the new vizier, but he died two months later. Nur al-Din appointed Saladin as Shirkuh's successor, but not because of his strengths. Historian James Reston Jr. says Saladin was picked because Nur al-Din "did not want a powerful competitor in Cairo, and he was certain that he could control his malleable and polite ward."[40]

Vizier

At thirty years old, Saladin was the new vizier of Egypt, and he immediately had his hands full. He had taken over a hostile country and had to win over the Egyptian people without becoming a threat to Nur al-Din back home. Saladin placed Syrian emirs, including three of his brothers and his father, in key Egyptian positions. He quelled a mutiny by the Nubian army (an Egyptian people), and he dealt with a Frankish attack on the Egyptian port of Damietta. In his first nine months as vizier, Saladin proved himself to be an organized, effective leader.

Nur al-Din then pressed Saladin to change Egypt from practicing the Shiite form of Islam to Sunni. Saladin did so in September 1171. Saladin himself would assume a more religious role from that point on. He now had a base (Egypt), and that meant armies and wealth with which to unite the lands of Islam. As Saladin's power increased, Nur al-Din grew jealous, worried that Saladin would no longer defer to him. When he demanded Saladin's help on a joint operation against crusader castles, Saladin turned him down. Nur al-Din's anger rose, and suddenly there was a threat that he might go to war against Saladin.

Saladin's father, Ayyub, gave his son wise advice, which made a lifelong impression on him. Always the negotiator, Ayyub warned Saladin that everyone's loyalty was owed to Nur al-Din. It was his land and they were all his slaves. He told Saladin that he should send Nur al-Din a message saying that there was no need to invade, such as "My Lord need but send a courier on a camel to lead me back to Syria by a turban cloth about my neck."[41] Ayyub advised his son that, when facing a powerful enemy, one should never provoke him, always try to appease him. But know that if the enemy did invade, they would all fight to the death.

Saladin did not fight Nur al-Din, nor did he have to negotiate, because Nur al-Din died suddenly on May 15, 1174. His eleven-year-old son succeeded him, but not for long. Saladin led his Egyptian army to Syria and took over. Now he was the sultan of Syria and Egypt, and he eyed the crusader kingdom that was pinched in the middle of his empire.

A United Islam

In the spring of 1175, Saladin, now thirty-eight years old, was named the king of Syria. The caliph in Baghdad also recognized him as the emperor of Syria and Egypt. In Islamic law, succession in leadership is different from in the West, where it is granted by either birthright or election. In Islam, the strongest is allowed to take control. Although Saladin had made some enemies, namely those loyal to Nur al-Din's family, he believed that he was the best man to lead Syria because his interest in the holy war was as passionate as Nur al-Din's. It was also accepted practice in Islam that "the conquest of a state was consummated by possession of the former monarch's wife or daughter."[42] Wisely, Saladin married Nur al-Din's widow, Ismat, gaining himself approval by the Syrians at large.

Saladin then returned to Cairo, choosing it as his center of power. He began building a society filled with colleges, public

Saladin believed he was destined to lead his subjects in holy war against the European crusaders.

works, and fortifications of the city walls. He wanted students to have free education and a good quality of life. His generosity inspired his subjects' loyalty. In his council meetings, Saladin demanded neither respect nor decorum. He encouraged everybody present to be honest and to speak freely. Consequently, no one was intimidated by him. He gained a reputation for being able to mediate conflicts rather than causing more bloodshed.

Saladin's quest to eliminate the crusader kingdom was renewed when he was surprise-attacked in 1177 by the Christian king Baldwin while out with a small party. The intruders charged down on his group, and Saladin was personally attacked by three knights. One of his guards cut them down and Saladin barely escaped. The Franks had broken a truce, leaving Saladin little choice but to go on the offensive against them. Saladin vowed to take back Jerusalem within a year. While he would work for the next ten years trying to unite Muslims of many dynastic differences, Saladin also began to form a plan against the crusaders.

Hattin and Jerusalem

But before Jerusalem came the town of Hattin. During the summer of 1187, after years of raids, skirmishes, truces, and broken truces with the Franks, Saladin mobilized the largest army in his history, consisting of about twelve thousand horsemen and twelve thousand foot soldiers. However, defeating the Franks at Hattin had more to do with strategy and weather than with brute force. Saladin prevented the Frankish army from reaching water, which, in the heat of July, proved to be deadly for the Franks. Heat exhaustion and dehydration set in, and Saladin's men set a brushfire to intensify the sun's powerful heat. Once the Frankish defeat was complete, their leaders were brought before Saladin. Showing his respect for their rank, he said to them, "Kings do not kill each other."[43] However, Saladin did order two hundred Templar and Hospitaller knights to be killed after they refused to convert to Islam. Ordinary soldiers were sold as slaves.

Saladin continued to take other cities in the region, including Acre, without opposition, for he offered generous terms: People could leave freely with their belongings and he would not kill anyone. Saladin then took Jerusalem on October 2 after besieging it for two weeks. It was a civilized takeover without any looting or violence. Saladin set ransoms for the Christian population and even paid some himself for those who had no money, once again demonstrating his generosity.

In a letter he wrote to the caliph, Saladin said, "For nearly a century, this city [Jerusalem] was in the hands of unbelievers and polluted by polytheism . . . and yet the wish to reconquer the city did not come to previous sovereigns, until the moment God chose me and called me to take it."[44]

The year 1187 was a glorious one for Saladin and the holy war. Some of the money raised by the ransoms at Jerusalem was spent to reestablish Muslim holy places. Saladin, as was typical of him, kept nothing for himself; he dispensed the remaining money to soldiers and emirs. The following summer, Saladin led his troops in taking Tortosa, Lattakia, and six more strongholds, making a serious dent in the Christian presence.

The Third Crusade

Saladin was not naive enough to think there would be no retaliation by the Western countries for his ambitions the last two years. He was now fifty years old, gray haired, and thin from battling a recurring illness that caused colic and fever. Saladin had several wives, which was allowed in Islam, and seventeen sons. He was a devoted father and regretted the time he spent away from his family because of war campaigning.

With the launching of the Third Crusade in 1190 by King Richard I of England and King Philip II of France, Saladin's life was about to become more difficult. The Franks chose the city of Acre as their first conquest. Before the two kings arrived, Conrad of Montferrat led a siege. He tried collapsing the walls using bombardment and fire, with no success. Saladin's forces withstood the onslaught, but not without strain. Saladin was having problems of his own keeping his nephew Taqi al-Din's army involved with the defense of Acre. Taqi al-Din wanted to leave and explore the possibility of establishing his own kingdom. When he did leave, he took up arms against some of Saladin's vassals. Saladin was furious that his nephew would abandon the holy war and then attack his own people for personal gain.

In the meantime, Philip II and Richard I arrived and built spectacular siege machines. Although Saladin was well aware that the two kings had conflicting interests in their homelands, he also knew they were powerful and arrogant men, especially Richard, making them worthy opponents. Richard made it clear that his goal was to reestablish a Christian kingdom and then return home. Saladin first tried to negotiate with the English king.

Saladin appointed his brother, al-Adil, as his negotiator. Nothing came of the negotiations, but al-Adil became friends with Richard I.

Saladin raises his arms in victory over a Christian enemy during the Third Crusade.

In fact, his son later became knighted by the English king. The siege went on, and when Saladin received fewer reinforcements than needed as a result of Taqi al-Din's desertion, the fall of Acre became imminent. Ignoring the chain of command, Saladin's commanders began to negotiate terms of surrender without him. His troops no longer wished to fight and accused him of destroying Islam.

On July 12, 1191, Saladin had no choice but to surrender Acre and agree to terms of paying the crusaders 200,000 dinars over a three-month period and handing over six hundred Christian prisoners. In return, all of the Muslims and their families were free to go. Understandably, Saladin was devastated over the loss of Acre. But for some reason, he did not stick to the payment schedule. This angered and frustrated Richard, who suspected that Saladin was delaying payment in order to prevent the crusaders from their ongoing campaign. This might have been true, for winter was approaching. It was to Saladin's advantage to rest his troops and refresh them for spring engagements. But it also may have been as simple a problem as a lack of funds.

Richard then did something that shocked the Muslim world. He ordered the execution of three thousand Muslim prisoners, including women and children. Newby says that "although Saladin was grieved and angered by the atrocity he would not have been shocked or surprised."[45] From then on, Saladin no longer showed mercy or kindness to his prisoners, but instead ordered their execution as well, even though it was not his way. But, according to Regan, "after the fall of Acre no Muslim garrison could be relied on to resist Richard. The very existence of the Lionheart seemed to diminish the morale of Saladin's troops."[46] The tide had turned on Saladin.

As Richard I systematically moved his troops south along the coast, defeating Saladin's army and taking back the cities of Arsuf and Jaffa, he seemed unstoppable. In contrast to Saladin's leadership style, Richard played the warrior himself with gusto, charging into skirmishes. As a result, his men followed with more enthusiasm and ambition than Saladin's. Saladin resorted to setting tarantulas loose at night in the crusaders' camp and shooting arrows at them by day. While Richard's army kept perfect discipline, Saladin observed them from a safe distance, searching for weaknesses. Finally, he planned to wait until the crusaders headed inland to Jerusalem, away from their water source, and in the heat of August, he hoped to surround them, as he had in Hattin. He also sent his troops to destroy Ascalon, a city just down the coast, to prevent Richard from winning it, thereby pushing the crusaders toward Jerusalem.

Even as Saladin planned his military strategy, his council sought to form a truce with Richard I. Saladin's health was more fragile than ever, and the Muslims were tired and wanted to go home. But Saladin was against peace, declaring, "If we make peace with these people, there is nothing to protect us against their treachery. . . .

The best thing to do is to persevere in the Holy War until we have either driven them all from the coast, or we ourselves die in the attempt."[47]

In the end, there was no battle over Jerusalem. Richard and the crusading army concluded that, even if they could take the city, the defense of it in the future would be endless, and none of the crusaders wished to live there permanently. In addition, Richard needed to return home to subdue Philip II's invasion of his lands. Richard and Saladin agreed to a truce on September 2, 1192, of three years and eight months. The crusaders would keep the cities they had already taken, and Christians would be allowed access to Jerusalem. The Muslims retained the territory they had gained. The Third Crusade was over.

Death

When Richard I left, Saladin was fifty-four years old. Saladin made his way to Damascus for the winter. He worried that war with the crusaders would resume one day, probably after his own death, and that Islam would never be as united under any of his sons as it was under him.

War weary and poverty stricken, Saladin nevertheless died a hero to his people.

In February 1193, Saladin was stricken with a chill and a fever. His biographer, Baha al-Din, wrote that, as Saladin awaited his servant to cool a scalding bath, the servant knocked the jug of cold water onto Saladin. Though some masters would behead a servant for such clumsiness, Saladin said, "My dear fellow, if you aim to kill me, give me due warning."[48] To his dying day, Saladin saw all Muslims equal in the eyes of God.

Saladin did not recover; he died on March 4, 1193. The people of Damascus grieved and mourned freely in the streets. Saladin died a poor man, and money had to be borrowed to pay for his funeral. He was buried in the palace garden during evening prayer.

During his final days, Saladin advised his eldest son to strive to be gentle instead of hostile. It would serve him well. Saladin was undoubtedly one of the dominant Muslim leaders of the twelfth century, taking over Egypt, uniting Islam, and opposing the crusaders; his moral character is what elevated him as a warrior and leader. Israeli historian Meron Benvenisti says of Saladin, "I think he deserves the admiration of a man like Richard the Lionheart and many Crusader knights who will believe that he is maybe even the ultimate example of knighthood of [the] Middle Ages."[49]

CHAPTER 5

Don Pero Niño, Chivalrous Knight

Don Pero Niño was a chivalrous knight, sea captain, and captain in the King's Guard in fourteenth-century Castile (a region of Spain). He was born to a noble family, raised in the privileged surroundings of a royal court, and followed the natural course of what would be expected of him—becoming a knight and a gentleman. He grew up with the pure intention of serving his king. During his twenties, Pero Niño's leadership capabilities led to an opportunity to lead his country in battles, as well as skirmishes on the seas. Through it all, he displayed physical strength, courage, and skill, which earned him renown. Pero Niño took knighthood and chivalry seriously, and strived to be the most courteous, Christian, merciful, loyal, and generous knight possible.

Childhood

Don Pero Niño was born in 1378 to a noble family in Castile. His father was descended from a French royal family, and his mother was from the house of La Vega, a great noble family of Castile. Historian D'A.J.D. Boulton says that Pero Niño enjoyed a privileged childhood in the royal household of the king of Castile because his "mother, Ines de la Vega . . . had been made the wet-nurse of the future Enrique III in 1379."[50] (Even though Ines de la Vega was a noblewoman, unlikely to become a wet nurse for another's child, Enrique III was a royal child entrusted to her care.) According to Pero Niño's biographer, Gutierre Diaz de Gamez, who was Pero Niño's flag bearer for many years, the future king adored the boy. Enrique and Pero Niño grew up as best friends.

Between the ages of ten and fourteen, Pero Niño was assigned a tutor who instructed him in the ways of Christianity and the manners required of a nobleman. Enrique came to the throne on his fourteenth birthday, in 1393. Boulton says Enrique "gave his own arms to his childhood companion Pero."[51] Pero Niño had turned fifteen, and with this armor, he began his training as a knight, jousting with lances and learning the skills of a bullfighter. He demonstrated talent and strength.

Three years later, when Pero Niño was eighteen, he distinguished himself in a battle in which, according to de Gamez, he "had borne himself so well . . . that thereafter men spoke much of him, praising him and accounting him the peer of good knights."[52] Pero Niño was a brave, skilled warrior and a nobleman, ready and willing to help his king. Enrique assigned him some troops to lead into Portugal, with whom he was at war. During the seventeen-day campaign, they sacked and burned the city of Viseo.

Young Knight

The following year, 1397, when he was nineteen, Pero Niño was to prove himself a formidable warrior. The Castilian region of Galicia turned away from Enrique, following instead the archbishop of Santiago, Don Juan Garcia. The archbishop took up a defensive position at the castle of Pontevedra. During the siege, Pero Niño fought tirelessly, even after being wounded. De Gamez says that "each of his blows was signal: from some did he shear a great part of their shields; others did he strike upon the head with his sword."[53] Pero Niño was struck in the neck with an arrow. Lances struck his shield, but he kept on advancing. He was also struck in the nose with a crossbow, "piercing his nostrils through most painfully, whereat he was dazed."[54] Nonetheless, he proceeded to the steps of the castle walls and cut through the enemy to enter, fending off his opponents' clubs. When both sides ceased fighting due to exhaustion, Pero Niño found his shield completely tattered, his sword hilt broken, the blade jagged, and his armor broken in a number of places.

At a tournament soon after, Pero Niño proved himself to be the top contender. De Gamez describes his appearance, saying that he had a well-formed body, not too tall or too short, strong legs, a hard fist, and a delicate waist. He had a pleasant voice and dressed very well. In fact, he dressed so well that others looked to him for fashion trends. Pero Niño also prided himself on being an expert on armor and horses. He trained different horses for different functions, such as war, parades, or jousting. Pero Niño seemed to be the epitome of knightly perfection: He was an excellent jouster and could throw a lance, darts, and the discus.

Pero Niño displayed chivalrous virtues as well. He was courteous, gracious, honest, and loyal to his king, and he defended the poor. He neither drank nor ate to excess, and he respected ladies

Pero Niño proved himself especially gifted in jousting competitions as well as in his adherence to the code of chivalry.

as a nobleman should. Pero Niño married Doña Costanza de Guevara, a beautiful young widow of noble lineage. They had a baby boy, whom they named Don Pedro. Like Pero Niño, his son entered the king's household. However, Doña Costanza died five years later.

Captain of the Seas

In 1404, when Pero Niño was twenty-six years old, the king was in need of a sea captain to defend the Castilian coastline against corsairs (local pirates) and Moors. As the sea captain, Pero Niño was given carte blanche to choose mariners, oarsmen, crossbowmen, and quartermasters to his liking. Paid in advance, and abundantly furnished with arms and supplies, Pero Niño and several galleys set sail. At first, they encountered nothing.

When they sighted a corsair fleet, they pursued them to the port of Marseilles. Here, the corsairs sought the protection of the pope, a resident of Marseilles. The pope offered to host a dinner for Pero Niño and his men in peace, and Pero Niño had no choice but to accept. During that night, the corsairs left Marseilles, and Pero Niño awoke quite ill with a fever. Whether or not it was foul play is unknown, but it was a convenient coincidence that Pero Niño was ill the day after his dinner with the pope.

Pero Niño was very angry to find the corsairs gone, and ordered his men to set sail in the face of an approaching storm. His sailors informed him that it was too dangerous, but de Gamez says that Pero Niño "took no account of any danger when it was a question of gaining honour, [and he] had so great a wish to catch these Corsairs, that he forgot all perils and toils which might befall."[55] The fleet left. Encountering strong gales and huge waves, they struggled to prevent the boats from sinking. They spent the night bailing and praying. Finally the storm passed, and they had all survived. As they approached the port of Alguer, they spotted three corsair ships. Pero Niño took back one of the ships, which had originally been stolen from Seville.

Pero Niño then ordered his fleet to sail along the Barbary Coast in search of other ships. As they approached the Port of Tunis, they discovered a Moorish fleet. During his attempt to board and steal a galley, Pero Niño found himself isolated on its deck, and he was forced to fight single-handedly. True to his character, seeing himself as an invincible knight defending his king's interests, Pero Niño fought wildly until he beat back many Moors. According to de Gamez, he "hurled himself upon them, fierce as a lion who throws himself upon his prey, striking, killing, driving them before him on to the deck."[56] Pero Niño did not walk away unscathed, however. He was severely injured from lances and arrows; particularly harmful was an arrow wound in his leg.

Once he reached a safe port, Pero Niño took time to repair the ships, pay his men, and have the wounded men treated. However, he ignored advice that his own leg injury needed medical attention. He was anxious to return to duty on the seas. After another expedition, though, it became clear that Pero Niño's wound had festered and was spreading infection throughout his body. Upon his return to Seville, Andrea Hopkins says that "his doctors advised amputation as the only way of saving his life."[57] Pero Niño refused, saying,

> If the hour when I must die is come, let it befall me as God wills. But for a knight it is better to die with all his limbs whole and united as God has given them to him, than to

live wretched and crippled, and to look at himself and see that he is good for nothing.[58]

The surgeons tried cauterizing the wound with a burning iron instead. But when it was hot enough, they feared hurting Pero Niño. Instead, he "took the glowing iron in his hand and himself moved it all over his leg."[59] Miraculously, the wound healed, and Pero Niño had a full recovery.

The Spanish engage the Moors in battle.

In 1405, Pero Niño set off on another mariner journey at the urging of his king. This time his fleet headed to England to help the French king fight their English enemy. Their mission was to capture English vessels. Richard Barber says that Pero Niño "saw nothing incompatible with chivalry in becoming captain of a galley in the Spanish fleet which was little more than a licensed corsair, raiding in reprisal the Barbary coast and the Mediterranean, as well as an expedition to Cornwall."[60] As far as Pero Niño was concerned, his duty was to serve his king. He did not need to justify his actions to anyone else. Pero Niño and his men proceeded to seek out undefended towns, go ashore, burn and pillage them, and fight anyone who tried to stop them. When it was time to winter, Pero Niño and his men were welcomed in France.

France

Treated like a gentleman and nobleman, Pero Niño was wined and dined in an admirable fashion by the French, and he enjoyed their companionship and culture. Barbara Tuchman says that he "left a picture of noble life as enchanted and bucolic in reality as it was often represented to be in tapestries."[61] For entertainment, they arranged jousting tournaments, at which Pero Niño's reputation brought honor to his country. He took all the prizes. Sometimes he fought against two opponents at a time, and he won against France's best knight and a renowned German one. As de Gamez writes, "thereafter Pero Niño was known to the whole court, and men held him in great account in all the seats of honour, and he was bidden to all the feasts that were given."[62]

Pero Niño, now twenty-eight and widowed, met a rich and beautiful French widow named Jeannette de Bellengues, with whom he fell in love. Pero Niño wished to marry her, but her father asked to delay a wedding for two years because Pero Niño was still officially campaigning in wars, and his daughter was respectfully required to mourn for some time yet. Pero Niño agreed to return in two years for his bride. He left France with his men to seek out more English ships.

Diplomat

Pero Niño sailed to Jersey, an island closer to France than to England. Inhabited historically by Bretons, the island was currently ruled by English knights. Pero Niño was determined to either capture the entire island or burn it to the ground. Joining forces with a number of French ships, Pero Niño organized a ground assault with all the men, Castilian and French. When the enemy lined up on the beach to resist them, he gave a gallant speech to his men:

> Now, my friends, you see how you are in the enemy's country. Look, there they are drawn up for battle, well armed and ready to come against us, just as we are to march against them. They are many, but they are neither so brave nor so strong as you. . . . Fight hard, do not let yourselves be beaten; be all firm and single-hearted.[63]

Both sides formed lines and then charged at each other with determination. The Castilians fought vigorously but made little gain. When they succeeded in killing the English general, however, the enemy broke down and began to run away. Pero Niño took the time to see to his wounded, reorganize the surviving men, and make sure everyone was fed. The next day, he announced to his men that they were going to either become masters of the island or burn it. He sent such a message to the city's leaders. He and a hundred knights approached the city, burning the villages they passed to demonstrate their resolve.

A wall fresco depicts a pair of jousting knights. Pero Niño demonstrated total resolve to uphold this knightly order.

What Pero Niño discovered was not what he expected, and he did not react in a standard military fashion. The people of Jersey told him they were Christians, just like the Castilians, and explained that they were ruled by the English not by choice but by force. They had no objection to Pero Niño's claiming Jersey for his own, as long as he did not kill everyone and burn everything in sight. Pero Niño listened to their appeal but condemned their alliance with the English to preserve peace. He insisted that they swear allegiance to him and give up their city to him. The people of Jersey stood firm, telling him that he would have to kill every man, woman, and child to have their city. But they would be more than willing to pay him a ransom to be left alone.

Pero Niño decided to accept this ransom proposal for a number of reasons. First, he wanted to show mercy on God's people. Second, he was going to receive plenty of money and booty that he could share with his men, enabling him to consider the expedition a success. And finally, he did not really want to fight these people and prolong his stay on Jersey because he knew that English ships would arrive any day to reinforce their garrison on the island. On this expedition, Pero Niño demonstrated great leadership skill, military might, and the ability to diplomatically negotiate the best solution.

Knighthood

Upon return to Madrid, Pero Niño went to visit King Enrique. The king was very proud of Pero Niño's accomplishments in aiding their French neighbor and announced that he wished to knight Pero Niño. Although Pero Niño had already been knighted in other countries, this was the first time he was to be officially knighted by his king in his country. According to Barber, he was "knighted in 1407 at the end of his chivalric career."[64] A feast followed the ceremony, celebrating Pero Niño's great contribution to Castile.

Soon afterward, King Enrique died, and his son Juan was proclaimed the new king. Since he was still a child, his mother, Queen Doña Catalina, and the late king's brother, Don Fernando, became regents. Pero Niño was planning to return to France, but the Moors began invading Castile. Pero Niño volunteered to lead an army against them.

Moorish Wars

Alongside Don Fernando, Pero Niño set off to war. They besieged and took a number of castles back from the Moors. As was his usual pattern, Pero Niño fought like a wildcat. When his lance broke, he resorted to his sword. When his horse was killed beneath him, he set out on foot. When a supply train was jeopardized, he marched on foot with others to protect it and eventually reached safety. When he returned to Spain, he was made a captain of the King's Guard. With this official title and position, Pero Niño knew he could not go to France, marry Jeannette de Bellengues, and take up residence there. He sent her word that he had to break their engagement.

Fall from Grace

At thirty-one years old, Pero Niño was so well known within Castile and the surrounding region for his gallantry and chivalry that he could have chosen any woman to be his wife and been warmly received. However, he chose Doña Beatriz, a woman already betrothed in a political alliance outside of Castile. Pero Niño risked everything he had for her, including his wealth and reputation. And he suffered the consequences.

Pero Niño fell in love with Doña Beatriz and successfully wooed her through third parties carrying messages, since the two could not actually meet. Her friends told her, "If he were not what he is, we should not thus praise him; but he is to-day, without question, the flower of all knights in nobility and in chivalry, and in all fair virtues, as much as could be the best knight in the world."[65] Pero Niño said he would love Doña Beatriz honorably and loyally and that she was the only woman in the world to whom he wished to offer this love. After Pero Niño convinced her brother of his love, who in turn talked to his sister, Doña Beatriz agreed to marry him. They were secretly betrothed, and de Gamez says that Pero Niño was never happier.

The marriage proposal was rejected, however, by Beatriz's father, who had other plans for her future. Pero Niño campaigned for his case, insisting that he loved Beatriz more than any man could love a woman and that, as an outstanding knight, he was worthy of such a lady; he begged her father to consent as a personal favor to him. Even though he continued to be rejected, Pero Niño refused to give up. He offered to settle the matter through a duel, for he would rather die than lose Beatriz. Pero Niño suggested that he take on two opponents at once, and if he should kill them both, Beatriz should be his with no further argument. The proposal was rejected.

The queen, fearful that Pero Niño would either be killed or be imprisoned for betrothing himself to Beatriz without permission,

The Moors surrender to the Spanish. Beatriz's father pardoned Pero Niño when he realized the knight would be needed to fight the Moors.

urged him to leave town and hide for a while. By following her advice, Pero Niño forfeited his position as captain of the King's Guard. He easily dodged his pursuers while Doña Beatriz was imprisoned in a palace for a year and a half. She swore that she would rather die than have any husband other than Pero Niño.

Eventually, the queen was able to convince her court that Castile could not afford to lose such a valuable knight and captain over such an issue. The Moors were creating more problems for Castile, and Pero Niño was needed. Beatriz's father agreed to pardon him and welcome him back.

Pero Niño was reestablished as captain in the King's Guard and given a lavish wedding. He spent the remaining years of his life serving his kingdom in the same noble spirit that he always had done. He died in 1454, at seventy-six years of age. Although Pero Niño's death is not recorded in de Gamez's biography, it is reasonable to assume that his funeral was an honorable affair.

Pero Niño's service to Castile as a knight was unequivocally loyal. He embraced all the qualities of chivalry and strived to emulate them. He undertook Castile's needs with pride, courage, and a leadership that served his men well, for at the end of every battle, he made sure his men were paid and taken care of. Pero Niño took better care of his men than he did of himself, as proven by the leg wound that almost cost him his life. The only time he ever disagreed with his superiors and risked his career was for love. And in the end, he succeeded in winning them over because they could not afford to lose their best knight.

CHAPTER 6

Bertrand du Guesclin, Soldier Knight

Bertrand du Guesclin was to France what William Marshal was to England. He was an extraordinarily talented knight, with a gift to lead and win battles, who came from a relatively poor family. He also died a national hero, and was respected by French royalty and nobility despite his lowly birth. But while Marshal was the flower of chivalry, Guesclin was a strong, brutal warlord. From aggressive childhood play to the last battle he fought, Guesclin displayed a violent character, which contributed to his becoming one of the most well-known and successful soldiers France ever had.

Childhood

Bertrand du Guesclin was born in 1320 to a French family of modest means in Brittany, France. Being the eldest son, he should have been raised with respect by his family. However, his parents were not very fond of him. Bertrand was physically violent from a young age. He was unattractive, "short and stocky, with broad shoulders and long arms," says historian Andrea Hopkins, "and all records of him agree in noting his remarkable ugliness."[66] His father beat him regularly, and once locked Bertrand in the dungeon. Bertrand's father was a Breton knight and disliked his son's vulgar ways, considering him a rascal and a clown. Historian Richard Barber claims that Bertrand's youthful escapades included "running away from home and leading a gang of the village youths."[67]

Despite receiving little nurturing from his parents, Bertrand grew up to be a successful soldier. Since other children despised him, he commanded their respect by becoming the strongest and toughest of them all. He played rough games, to his father's displeasure, and according to Tim Newark, "he was a bully and a thug."[68] Although this behavior did not lend well to gaining popularity, it laid the groundwork for great success in the tournament circuit. By the time Bertrand was twenty-one, he was well known for his ability to wrestle and joust. He needed a job in which he could put his violent nature to good use.

Freelance Guerrilla Leader

The 1340s brought civil war to Brittany. The line of succession was under dispute between the late duke's niece, Jeanne de Penthievre, who was married to the nephew of the king of France, and the late duke's half-brother, the count of Montfort, who sought help from the king of England. Guesclin supported Jeanne's claim and built his own band of soldiers, paying them with his mother's jewels. Relying on tactics that included ambush and trickery, Guesclin earned a reputation for getting the job done by whatever means necessary. Newark describes a successful attack in 1350 in which Guesclin "disguised 60 of his followers as wood-cutters. They burst into the castle of Fougeray while its English commander was away plundering. As the English returned, Guesclin ambushed them."[69] In the face of the massive French defeat in 1346 at the battle of Crécy, in which the English thoroughly decimated the French army by use of the longbow, Guesclin's approach to warfare was both practical and necessary for victory.

A portrait of Bertrand du Guesclin, whose violent nature was apparent from an early age.

Guesclin earned his knighthood in 1354, when he led thirty archers and ambushed an approaching English army intending to raid a French banquet at the castle of Montmuran. Guesclin even managed to capture a hundred English soldiers and their famous captain, Hugh of Calveley. Guesclin became a paid knight in the service of Jeanne and her husband, Charles de Blois.

Knight

Guesclin's violent, impulsive character served him well under war conditions. In 1356, when his own brother, Olivier, was captured by an English knight during a truce, he was enraged at this violation of the code of chivalry. He boldly rode into the English camp, stated his complaint to the duke of Lancaster, and demanded that honor be satisfied. A duel was arranged. On the day of the duel, the English knight Thomas of Canterbury wanted to avoid the fight and offered to release Olivier. But Guesclin was not satisfied. He replied, "If [Canterbury] will not fight, let him surrender to my mercy and present his sword to me, holding it by the point."[70] The duel proceeded.

On horseback, the men crashed into each other. Guesclin dismounted and threw away his sword. Canterbury charged at him with clear advantage. Newark writes,

> The English horse reared, Guesclin lunged at its belly with his dagger. The horse crashed to the ground with Canterbury beneath it. Guesclin rushed over to the knight, ripped open his visor and battered the stunned Englishman with his armoured fists.[71]

Guesclin spared him, but won the freedom of his brother, a purse from Lancaster, Canterbury's arms and armor, and most important, the respect of the English.

Guesclin further established himself as a warrior during the long siege at Rennes. Lancaster built a siege machine to try to penetrate the French castle. Guesclin placed five hundred archers on the castle walls and they shot flaming arrows at the siege engine, successfully burning it to the ground. Eventually, another truce was arranged, and the English were ordered to leave. Guesclin was given the lordship of La Roche-Derrien and made a knight banneret, a more prestigious position, as a reward for his defense of Rennes. Dauphin Charles (acting for his captured father, the French king) granted Guesclin an annual income and a pension of two hundred pounds and assigned him the rank of captain of Pontorson, a town in need of defense from the king of Navarre.

Captain

En route to Pontorson, Guesclin witnessed a ravaged French countryside. Since 1360, when the Treaty of Bretigny was signed and the war between England and France ceased, thousands of unemployed English soldiers had been left with no income. Since so many French nobles had died in the battles of Crécy and Poitiers, there were few obstacles to keep these English mercenaries from looting any towns they chose. They were, in effect, causing more havoc in France now than they had when they were under the English king's command. At least then, organized skirmishes and sieges were expected. Guesclin was furious and vowed to do what he could to stop the mercenaries from such activity and restore peace for the peasants of the countryside: "By God! 'Tis far worse, even, than ever I had thought! It must not be suffered to go on, and by all that is Holy I swear I will avenge these poor people!"[72] While Guesclin was a ferocious warrior, he held dear the knightly virtues of protecting the poor and innocent.

It was around this time that Guesclin is said to have married Tiphaine, a beautiful, cultured daughter of a wealthy nobleman. They had known each other for some time, but Guesclin was constantly engaged in battle somewhere. Although they would rarely be together, Guesclin's marriage to Tiphaine was a happy one.

Pontorson was a frontier town between Brittany and Normandy. The king of Navarre, Charles the Bad, held lands in Normandy, and was challenging the dauphin for the throne of France. Guesclin arrived in Pontorson with an army of fifteen hundred men. With an orderly formation of archers in front protected by shielded warriors, the men opened battle with the Navarrese. In the hand-to-hand combat that followed, Guesclin's men slaughtered the Navarrese. At forty-two years old, Bertrand du Guesclin had proven himself a formidable military leader for his country. He was made count of Longueville as reward for his services. The dauphin also gave him the Chateau de Roche-Tesson in Normandy for his own.

During the next two years, Guesclin and his men sought out mercenary companies, either through siege or ground assault. The peasants came to adore Guesclin, for his actions freed them from the mercenary companies pillaging their villages and crops.

Captive

In 1364, the problem of succession in Brittany was still unresolved. The Montfort heir decided to besiege the town of Auray, which was loyal to Charles de Blois. Guesclin was asked to help Blois in the capacity of chief military adviser. He split the army into three divisions and a rear guard. He led one and Blois led another. The Montfort army appeared in a similar formation. At first, the armies were well matched. But during the battle, Blois and many of his knights were killed, and the remainder of his division dispersed. Guesclin's men were outnumbered and surrounded. Guesclin decided to surrender because, according to historian Shirley Carr, it was his "creed that a knight could best serve his cause, not by vainglorious death when all was lost, but by giving himself up, paying his ransom, and returning to the field."[73]

Guesclin's army lost nine hundred men that day as well as their beloved duke. Montfort was given the title and lands of Brittany by Charles V, now the king of France. In the

Charles II, the king of Navarre, is seen kneeling in prayer. Guesclin was charged with protecting Pontorson from the king's armies.

interest of leading the French army into yet another conflict, Charles V paid Guesclin's ransom.

Spain

New conflict arose in Spain in 1365. Charles V's sister-in-law, Blanche of Bourbon, was married to Don Peter the Cruel of Castile. Don Peter was known to be a tyrant who had troublemakers assassinated or imprisoned. When Blanche died, Charles suspected foul play. In addition, Don Peter was challenging the king of Aragon for the throne. Yet another rival, Don Henry, asked Charles to back his claim to the throne. Pope Urban V called for the expedition in Castile to be a Crusade because he knew that Don Peter had Muslims in his army. Guesclin, named the supreme military commander, recruited thirty thousand mercenaries to form the White Company, who all bore white crosses on their vests. Their mission was to overthrow Don Peter.

Guesclin encountered no difficulty in Castile, as Don Peter cowardly hid himself and his men put up little resistance. The conflict ended swiftly. Don Henry was crowned king and he generously gave lands and estates to Guesclin in gratitude. However, victory was short-lived. Don Peter soon fled to gain a new ally, the king of England's son, the Black Prince. In February 1367, the Black Prince arrived with twenty-five thousand men. As the two armies engaged in battle, the English army outfought Guesclin's, and he was soon surrounded. Guesclin surrendered.

The Black Prince was hesitant to accept ransom for Guesclin's freedom, concerned that Guesclin would return leading French soldiers against the English on some other battlefield. After being held for eight months, Guesclin begged him to reconsider, accusing the prince of being more afraid of him than of any other French soldier. The prince said, "Fix your own ransom and you shall be released forthwith."[74] Guesclin offered one hundred thousand crowns, the greatest sum of money ever paid for ransom. The prince said it was too much and that Guesclin would never be able to raise the money. Guesclin proudly retorted, "The King . . . will lend me what I lack, and there is not a spinning-wench in all France who would not work her fingers off to gain for me what is necessary to win my freedom."[75] By New Year's Day 1368, all of the money was raised and Guesclin was released, illustrating his worth to Charles V and all of France.

In one last battle between Don Peter and Don Henry, Guesclin helped Don Henry to finally cut down Don Peter and his Muslim forces. Don Peter was killed, and the succession dispute over Castile came to an end. Don Henry gave Guesclin estates in the area, named him constable of Castile, and tried to proclaim him king of Granada. But Guesclin was called to France by Charles V for more pressing matters.

Constable of France

Since the Treaty of Bretigny ten years before, Charles V had taken advantage of the official truce between France and England to prepare his country for more war with England. France eventually wanted to reclaim all the lands in France that England held. Charles created a royal navy, built new walls around Paris, trained his soldiers in archery (since this weapon had been successfully used by the English at Crécy and Poitiers against the French), and reorganized the army into companies. Now he needed a constable,

A painting shows Guesclin, seated, in his position as constable of France.

a supreme commander of all the French armed forces. He chose Guesclin. Guesclin objected, however, because of his lowly birth, saying,

> My lord and noble King, . . . I am of too low blood to ac-
> cept the great office of Constable of France. Whoever ac-
> cepts it must command the most noble men as well as the

ordinary. How could I be so bold to order these lords here, your cousins and relations? Envy should be so great that I would fear it.[76]

The king insisted that no one would disobey Guesclin and that he must accept the position. So, at age fifty, Guesclin was invested in the office of constable.

Guesclin began the campaign against England by capturing the town of Poitiers. He proved himself to be a brilliant commander. Hopkins says he "put into action a plan of gradual erosion of English territories; while they conducted their traditional raiding parties, he retaliated by achieving more substantial gains of castles and towns. Gradually the English were pushed back towards the west coast. Du Guesclin seemed unstoppable."[77] Guesclin avoided engaging the English directly in any battle, and instead relied on the guerrilla tactics that had worked so well for him over the years. Guesclin and his men harassed the English army with archers whenever possible, raided their baggage trains, and held out in comfortable castles while the English soldiers camped in bad weather. "I do not say that the English should not be fought, . . . but I want it to be executed from a position of advantage," said Guesclin. "That is what the English did at Poitiers and Crecy."[78] Little by little, the English army weakened, and in 1376, when the Black Prince died from an illness, a truce was settled.

While Guesclin had been pursuing the English, his wife, Tiphaine, died. He had been looking forward to retirement in Spain where he could spend quiet, domestic days with her, uninterrupted. It was not to be. At the urging of Charles V, he remarried, choosing Jeanne, the daughter of Lord de Laval and Isabeau de Tintenac.

With the English subdued, Charles V decided to invade Brittany to try to remove Jean de Montfort from the duchy, since Montfort was loyal to the English. Guesclin strongly disagreed with this plan, because he did not want to make war in his place of birth. Even though Montfort was not the preferred duke, Guesclin would still be fighting other Bretons, his fellow countrymen. But he was caught between two sides. The Bretons already considered Guesclin a traitor to be serving Charles V. And now the king and his court acknowledged Guesclin's resistance to carrying out the king's wishes.

Guesclin was offended that the king would think of him as a traitor after all that he had done for the monarchy and France. He immediately resigned from his post and surrendered his sword. He decided to retreat to his lands in Spain and live a comfortable, quiet retirement. However, Charles apologized for insulting Guesclin and insisted he take back his sword and post of constable. Guesclin did so, and proceeded on his mission, which would be his last.

Death

As Guesclin and his army were besieging Chateau-neuf-de-Randon, he became ill. Realizing that he would not recover, Guesclin made a will and had a priest deliver him the sacraments of the church. He called some of the men to his bedside and said, "Remember, as I have exhorted you a thousand times, that wherever you are at war, the clergy, the women, the children, and the poor are not your enemies. Cherish and protect them."[79] To his king, he said, "Tell the king I am grieved not to have served him longer, but I could not have served him more faithfully."[80] On July 13, 1380, Bertrand du Guesclin, constable of France, died. He was sixty years old.

At Guesclin's request, his heart was buried next to his first wife, Tiphaine, in Dinan, but Charles V insisted that the rest of his body be buried with highest honors in Paris, at the Church of St. Denis, where he himself would be buried. Guesclin's death was kept as quiet as possible in order to conceal the great warlord's passing from France's enemies. Nine years later, King Charles VI held a splendid funeral service in his honor.

Bertrand du Guesclin's career as a soldier for France was a distinguished one, as he rose from an abusive childhood to become a knight, constable of France, and a national hero. He was respected by not only royalty, nobility, and peasants but his enemies as well. Newark reports that in French art and literature, Guesclin's name "was added to the list of chivalric heroes known as the Nine Worthies,"[81] ranking him with Alexander, Caesar, Arthur, and Charlemagne. Guesclin served knighthood when practical: He was unconditionally loyal to the French Crown, giving up the pursuit of a personal life for the king, and although he could be a brutal warrior, he always showed concern and mercy for the common people and clergy. However, his life witnessed the changing role of the knight from that of a chivalric soldier charging into battle in the name of glory to that of a more cunning, pragmatic warrior in pursuit of victory. Changing military tactics, such as the use of the longbow, demanded that the chivalric knight change too. Bertrand du Guesclin was a brilliant

Upon Guesclin's death, Charles V insisted that his body be interred with honors at the Church of St. Denis in Paris (pictured).

soldier for France, leading the country to glory many times, because he had the best qualities of a knight—bravery, loyalty, compassion, and strength. More important, he changed the way the French fought. As Hopkins says, "He foreshadowed the professional soldier of later centuries."[82]

CHAPTER 7

Sir John de Hawkwood, Mercenary

John de Hawkwood, like William Marshal, was not a firstborn son and would inherit nothing from his family. It is that much more impressive then that he emerged from working-class surroundings to become the captain general of Florence, Italy. When he died, Florence gave him a state funeral and erected a monument to him, which still hangs in its cathedral today. But Hawkwood, although a knight, did not rise to such fame and fortune because he was the epitome of chivalry. On the contrary, he lived during the fourteenth century when chivalry was not winning wars. Hawkwood trained as a soldier under Edward III, and when peace came, he had few alternatives other than becoming a mercenary, a soldier for hire. Although he exhibited courage, wisdom, generosity, and loyalty, they were never for any purpose other than monetary gain. He did seem to have a stronger code of ethics than other mercenary leaders, but his actions were never based on gaining the honor and glory for which knights struggled. Hawkwood's motives were victory and profit.

Childhood

John de Hawkwood was the sixth child born to Gilbert de Hawkwood, a tanner with a feudal dependence on the earl of Oxford in Essex, England. Of the five other children, four were girls and one was a boy, the heir to the family estate. The Hawkwoods were greatly relieved by the birth of a second son in 1320 because their firstborn son was often ill. Anticipating his early demise, Gilbert gave the new baby the same name, John, and the brothers became known as John the elder and John the younger. Following the birth of a third son, Nicholas, John's mother died. But surprising them all, John the elder survived childhood.

John the younger was a heavy-set and strong boy, with chestnut hair and brown eyes. At nine years old, he was taller than John the elder. He had a vigorous temperament that was well suited for plowing the fields and playing around with a sword and mace, but he had little interest in the family tannery, a business that converted cowhide into leather. He did his share of work but was far more interested in warriors and battle.

In a feudal society, since the eldest son inherits the family estate, subsequent sons have to find alternate means to support themselves. One avenue open to young men was the clergy. Another was knighthood. A visiting Templar knight named Sir Albrecht influenced John the younger. The Templar predicted the death of chivalry because it valued glory over victory. England had already defeated the Scots once, under the leadership of Edward I, not through the use of charging knights but with the longbow. The new King Edward III (who came to the throne when John was seven), although a supporter of chivalry, found his knights to be ineffective against marauding Scots. He too employed the use of archers and successfully defeated the Scots. John the younger would remember the value of the longbow and the importance of victory in war, no matter what the cost.

English Soldier

Gilbert died when John the younger was nineteen. As expected, John received nothing of consequence from his father's estate. But he was not disappointed. He knew this day was coming, and he prepared to join Edward III's army, which was fighting a war in France that would turn out to be the Hundred Years' War.

Hawkwood had already trained a little under his uncle's guidance. He asked John de Vere, the earl of Oxford, to take him along on his next campaign with the king. As a king's soldier, Hawkwood would be paid wages for half of each year, but he had to support himself for the other half. He resorted to leather repair and fared well enough.

Hawkwood withstood the rigorous training with little trouble; he was strong and focused. He wanted to be as effective a soldier as he could be. Within three years, Hawkwood was already a seasoned soldier, and he fought in the battle at Crécy in 1346. With superior strategy and force, the English won an overwhelming victory over the French at Crécy, losing only two hundred men to France's fifteen thousand.

A year later, tragedy struck. The Black Death (the bubonic plague) bore down upon Europe. France and England were ravaged by the rat-borne plague, which killed one person out of every three. The plague showed no favoritism: It took children as well as the elderly, women as well as men, priests as well as laypeople, nobles as well as the poor. Author Joseph Jay Deiss says that "John Hawkwood's luck was with him, and while his mates collapsed around him, he was spared."[83] Since so many nobles and leaders had died, the door opened for survivors to assume their coveted positions. Hawkwood became the leader of a small company under the Black Prince (Edward III's son).

War resumed six years after the Black Death, and Hawkwood led his company in the great battle at Poitiers, another English victory. The Black Prince was so impressed with Hawkwood that he ordered his knighthood. According to Deiss, "From the king himself, the country boy from Sible Hedingham received the golden spurs of knighthood. Sir John Hawkwood was ready now to fulfil his ordained career."[84] For the first time in his life, Hawkwood was not only a noble and a leader, but he was included in events open to nobles. He found himself at the Black Prince's table and exposed to wealth he had never before experienced. However, four years later, in 1360, the Treaty of Bretigny put an end to the war between England and France, and Hawkwood found himself without a job. Since most soldiers were professional warriors with

The defeated King John of France offers his sword to Edward III of England at the Battle of Poitiers. John de Hawkwood was knighted for his valiant performance in the English victory.

no landholdings at home to return to, the lack of war left them with few options. The one that made the most sense was to form their own companies of soldiers for hire. Hawkwood joined one of these.

Mercenary Captain

Hawkwood joined the White Company, a company of thirty-five hundred horsemen and another two thousand foot soldiers, who all wore white coats and plain armor and bore white banners. Led by a German knight, Albert Sterz, they made their way to Italy, where small wars were raging. Members of mercenary companies in Italy came to be known as condottieri, referring to the contracts used to engage such soldiers. Deiss says that the soldiers "were disciplined in battle, but highly undisciplined in camp. They were negligent, disorderly, rowdy; they carried with them much wine and many whores."[85] In her book *Knights*, author Andrea Hopkins also describes the mercenaries' conduct:

> Many chroniclers record the devastation that was left behind in a countryside . . . after an army of such men had passed through, describing it as a desert, uninhabited, uncultivated, with towns and villages burned and left to rot, and fields which had been full of crops or pasture rank with weeds and young trees.[86]

Hawkwood could not read or write, let alone speak Latin, the universal European language. So, he started to learn it. The Italians could not pronounce his name, so they elected to give him a new one, an Italian name. They chose "Giovanni Acuto," which translates to "John the Sharp." Soon after Hawkwood arrived in Florence, where there was a war going on between it and the city of Pisa, the Pisans hired the White Company. The Florentines hired a German mercenary company, and the two armies fought each other for several months. Hawkwood urged the men to demand more money from the Pisans, because he knew the Pisans were completely dependent on the White Company. They asked and were given six months' pay, spoils of the battle, free passage throughout Pisa, and winter quarters in the city. Deiss says that "in their enthusiasm, the men deposed the German Sterz to second in command, and elected Hawkwood in his place."[87] Now Hawkwood was in charge of his own company. He was Giovanni Acuto, captain general of the troops.

In the spring, Hawkwood surrounded Florence with his company. Even with its German mercenaries, Florence was outnum-

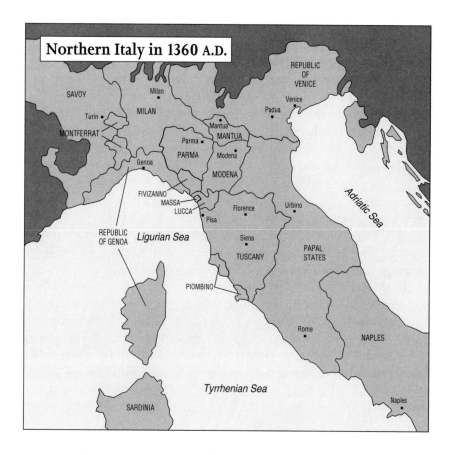

Northern Italy in 1360 A.D.

SAVOY

Turin •

MONTFERRAT

Milan •
MILAN

Genoa
Parma •
PARMA

Mantua
MANTUA

Modena •
MODENA

REPUBLIC
OF
VENICE

Venice •

Padua •

FIVIZANNO
MASSA
LUCCA •
Pisa •

Florence •

Urbino •

Adriatic Sea

REPUBLIC
OF GENOA

Ligurian Sea

Siena •
TUSCANY

PAPAL
STATES

PIOMBINO

Rome •

NAPLES

Tyrrhenian Sea

Naples

SARDINIA

bered and outmaneuvered by the White Company. But Florentine secret agents bribed some members of the White Company into deserting the Pisan cause, to which they agreed for a certain amount of gold. Hawkwood was bitter and angry that his men would desert a cause and desert him. According to Hopkins, "Though the condottieri were generally notorious for changing sides if someone made them a better offer, Hawkwood at least was concerned for his professional reputation and enjoyed much respect for his fidelity to his word."[88] Only eight hundred men remained with Hawkwood, but they were a loyal eight hundred men. As the conflict continued, Hawkwood developed a spy network to enhance his ability to strategize, and he promised his men double pay for a month if they beat the Florentines in the next battle. However, they lost, and the Florentines took two thousand Pisan prisoners. Hawkwood retreated with his company.

Defeat in one conflict did not, however, dictate failure in the next. Hawkwood's spy network came in handy in light of the fickle nature of the Italians. One day Hawkwood worked for one city, the next day another. He tried to keep abreast of the subtleties among them that could give him an advantage. Hawkwood's company was hired for many engagements over the next several years, the success of which earned it wealth and reputation. With that wealth he built up his company once again.

In response to the rise of mercenary companies, Pope Urban V eventually urged all honest men to fight against the mercenaries, calling them villains who terrorized innocent people. The once chivalrous knight had deteriorated to nothing more than an armed bully. The pope also implored the mercenaries themselves to take up the Cross and fight in a new Crusade. Then he threatened excommunication if they did not. But his appeals fell on deaf ears. Knights were no longer enticed to achieve glory from the church or anybody else. The pope was already unpopular and had several enemies, one of whom was Bernabo Visconti, known as a tyrant's tyrant. Bernabo's family was from Milan, which was historically a fief of the Holy Roman emperor. Bernabo wanted to break away from the pope and the emperor, desiring to build his own kingdom. He hired Hawkwood in an operation against the pope. Hawkwood would soon suffer the lowest point in his career: He was captured and imprisoned by papal forces. But as soon as his ransom was paid and he was freed, Hawkwood immediately returned to his company. Bernabo's next goal was to capture Florence.

The Florentines somehow learned of Bernabo's plan, and were well fortified with plenty of soldiers when Hawkwood's army arrived. During the night, Hawkwood's company endured a surprise attack from the Florentines. But Hawkwood was not in the habit of relying only on force. As Deiss explains, he resorted to a clever ambush:

> Half-armed, [Hawkwood's company] met with lances the Florentine vanguard of 400 horses. While his men at the barricades fought the vanguard, Hawkwood pretended flight by sending the pages on horseback to a ford, simultaneously stationing his best men in ambush. The Florentines sent 800 horses along the river to pursue. As their heavily weighted horses sank into the soft mud, Hawkwood's men in ambush closed a pincers. Many nobles, many knights, 2,000 men and 2,000 horses were taken prisoner. Hawkwood had redeemed himself.[89]

For the next two years, Hawkwood worked steadily for Bernabo. But when Bernabo decided to reduce his pay, Hawkwood consid-

After he was insulted by his employer, Bernabo Visconti, Hawkwood pledged loyalty to Bernabo's enemy, Pope Gregory XI (pictured).

ered it a breach of contract. As revenge, he chose to go to work for Bernabo's worst enemy: the church. "For his employer, Pope Gregory XI," says Deiss, "he formed a new and powerful Holy Company, composed of 1,500 lances [and] 500 archers."[90] Hawkwood was now fifty-five years old and the father of two sons. No recorded marriage is known, however.

The Holy Company

Always interested in earning large sums of money, Hawkwood allowed the Florentines to buy him off and prevent him from sacking their city, which was on the church's list. They paid him 130,000 gold florins to bypass Florence for three months. He proceeded to lead the Holy Company throughout Tuscany, collecting more monetary bribes from cities wishing to be left alone. Mean-

Hawkwood (pictured) put family ties above his church mercenary duty when his sons were held hostage, giving up his invasion of Bologna to save their lives.

while, the church was paying him thirty thousand florins a month to do its bidding. Hawkwood had no trouble playing both sides of a conflict when he could. He became a landowner for the first time when the church, behind in its pay schedule, awarded him "the lordship of Bagnacavallo, Cotignola, and Conselice—two towns and a village in the flat and fertile Romagna between Bologna and Rimini."[91]

In 1375, Hawkwood's two sons were kidnapped and held as hostages by Bologna, a city he was invading on behalf of the church. Hawkwood was furious but gave up the fight. According to Deiss,

> He abandoned the campaign against Bologna, and to retrieve the boy-hostages, agreed not only to a sixteen-month truce, but restored every prisoner he had captured and every head of cattle taken as spoil.
>
> For once he seemed to have enough of war. With his sons dressed like young princes and riding blooded ponies, he withdrew to his estates. There for more than a year he worked at building a great house, peacefully tending his lands like any English squire.[92]

Then, however, the cardinal summoned Hawkwood to pillage the small town of Cesena. Hawkwood became increasingly annoyed with his employers for falling behind on payments and was somewhat disenchanted with the cardinal's orders. To make an example of Cesena, the cardinal had ordered Hawkwood to slaughter all of the residents and completely plunder the town. "For three days and nights," says historian Barbara Tuchman, "beginning February 3, 1377, while the city gates were closed, the soldiers slaughtered."[93] Hawkwood's forces usually fought other armies. Now he was being ordered by the church to kill defenseless people. Hawkwood followed through on these orders but saved a thousand women, sending them to another town for safety. Even though he was a mercenary, he preferred to make money from the wealthy fighting the wealthy. He believed that killing innocent and impoverished people was pointless and cruel. So, when his old friend and enemy Bernabo Visconti approached him to join an antipapal league, Hawkwood was more than ready to listen.

Marriage

Bernabo offered to give Hawkwood his beautiful daughter Donnina for his wife as part of the deal. Hawkwood was now approaching the age of sixty and more than twice the age of the bride. However, Deiss says that he "still led his troops with the vigour of a young man" and was a man "of impressive presence, bronzed by the sun like an Italian."[94] Donnina was the daughter of Bernabo's most treasured mistress, Porina, and was his favorite. Bernabo hoped that bringing Hawkwood into the family as his son-in-law would guarantee the mercenary's allegiance. The wedding was held in 1377 and was a lavish affair. Hawkwood and Donnina would have three daughters, Zannetta, Caterina, and Anna.

The marriage alliance did not prove fruitful for Bernabo, however. Bernabo's wife, Regina, disliked Hawkwood and urged her husband to cancel his contract, which he did. Hawkwood then approached the Florentines and proposed that they hire him for 250,000 florins a year for his protection. He had uncovered a conspiracy plan to take over their city, which he promised to reveal to them if they hired him. They did so, caught the conspirators, and two years later, voted him the captain general of the Republic of Florence. Hawkwood's spy network earned him a comfortable pension.

Captain General

Hawkwood's installment as captain general in 1380 was received in Florence with great ceremony, followed by an elaborate feast. The city bought him a house (exempt from property tax), gave him more money in addition to his annual fee, and hoped he would live there with his wife and children. "For his remaining two decades," says Tuchman, "Hawkwood lived in riches and respect."[95]

In 1390, Bernabo's rebellious nephew, Gian Galeazzo Visconti, decided to conquer Florence. Hawkwood once again resorted to smart tactics. After boldly advancing to the battlefield with his company, expecting another mercenary company to join his, Hawkwood found himself alone. His army of seven thousand was completely outnumbered by Gian's twenty-six thousand. Hawkwood knew he had to retreat, but he also knew he would not be able to retreat fast enough with two major rivers to ford. He led his men to a ruined castle by one of the rivers, where they rested for four days. On the fifth day, they charged out of the castle and broke through the enemy's ranks. Then, Hawkwood successfully fooled Gian, as Deiss explains:

> Hawkwood sent "Zuzzo the trumpeter" with a blood-stained gauntlet to Verme, challenging Gian's army to battle on the following day. But on the coming of darkness,

Hawkwood quietly broke camp, leaving empty tents with banners flying, and a group of trumpeters with instructions to blow reveille as usual at daybreak. At intervals along the route of his retreat he shrewdly left wagons and asses loaded with booty—the surest way to slow the advance of mercenary soldiers.[96]

Hawkwood brought his men safely home and was the hero of Florence.

The Florentines were so impressed with Hawkwood's resourcefulness that they awarded him more money, gave each of his daughters a dowry, gave a pension to his wife, and offered to make the family Florentine citizens. Now in his seventies, Hawkwood arranged for his two older daughters to marry well. Zannetta, now fifteen, was given to Brezaglia, count of Porcia. Caterina, fourteen, was married to a soldier, Konrad Prospergh.

Death

Even though Hawkwood had made a stable and prosperous life for himself and his family in Florence, he considered returning to England. The place of his birth beckoned him. The Florentines had already voted to celebrate his life after his death by constructing a magnificent tomb for their hero. They did not want him to leave, but understood his desire to return to his birthplace. Before he could begin the journey, however, Hawkwood suffered a stroke and died on March 17, 1394. He was seventy-four years old.

After his death, his adopted countrymen of Florence gave Sir John de Hawkwood a lavish funeral in the Italian walled city.

The Florentines gave him a state funeral and commissioned an equestrian painting of Hawkwood on the wall of their cathedral. The English king, Richard II, who had never met Hawkwood but had heard of his fame, asked that his body be sent back to England for burial in a parish church.

Sir John de Hawkwood was never a ruler. He was never even a feudal lord. He had no desire to be. But at the height of his career as a mercenary captain, most of Italy worshiped him. He was richer than many nobles and kings, and he earned all of it from a company he guided with wisdom and skill. Though Hawkwood was knighted, and valued and demonstrated most knightly virtues, he was never an advocate of chivalry if it meant that a warrior had to sacrifice victory for honor and glory. He considered victory the ultimate reward, and made no apologies for pursuing it. As a mercenary, Hawkwood achieved enormous success, and as a general, exhibited military genius.

NOTES

Introduction

1. Quoted in Andrea Hopkins, *Knights*. London: Quarto, 1990, pp. 70–71.

Chapter 1: The Medieval Knight and His World

2. Hopkins, *Knights*, pp. 35, 38.

3. Hopkins, *Knights*, p. 125.

4. Hopkins, *Knights*, p. 144.

5. Richard Barber, *The Knight and Chivalry*. New York: Harper & Row, 1982, p. 159.

6. Hopkins, *Knights*, p. 113.

7. Hopkins, *Knights*, p. 74.

8. Quoted in Georges Tate, *The Crusaders: Warriors of God*. New York: Harry N. Abrams, 1996, p. 131.

9. Quoted in Tate, *The Crusaders*, p. 131.

10. Tate, *The Crusaders*, p. 30.

11. Tate, *The Crusaders*, p. 87.

Chapter 2: William Marshal, Loyalty Above All Else

12. Quoted in Georges Duby, *William Marshal: The Flower of Chivalry*. Translated by Richard Howard. New York: Pantheon Books, 1985, p. 25.

13. Quoted in Duby, *William Marshal*, p. 63.

14. Sidney Painter, *William Marshal: Knight-Errant, Baron, and Regent of England*. Baltimore, MD: Johns Hopkins Press, 1933, pp. 21–22.

15. Painter, *William Marshal*, p. 35.

16. Painter, *William Marshal*, p. 107.

17. Painter, *William Marshal*, p. 107.

18. Quoted in Duby, *William Marshal*, p. 150.

19. Duby, *William Marshall*, p. 6.

20. Painter, *William Marshal*, p. 285.

21. Quoted in Duby, *William Marshal*, p. 26.

Chapter 3: Richard the Lionheart, Crusader King

22. Geoffrey Regan, *Lionhearts*. New York: Walker, 1998, p. 2.

23. John Gillingham, *Richard the Lionheart*. New York: Times Books, 1978, p. 31.

24. Regan, *Lionhearts*, p. 3.

25. Gillingham, *Richard the Lionheart*, p. 64.

26. Gillingham, *Richard the Lionheart*, p. 69.

27. Regan, *Lionhearts*, p. 12.

28. Quoted in Gillingham, *Richard the Lionheart*, p. 120.

29. Quoted in James Reston Jr., *Warriors of God: Richard the Lionheart and Saladin in the Third Crusade*. New York: Doubleday, 2001, p. 97.

30. Regan, *Lionhearts*, p. 23.

31. Quoted in Reston, *Warriors of God*, p. 103.

32. Quoted in Gillingham, *Richard the Lionheart*, p. 161.

33. Quoted in Reston, *Warriors of God*, p. 230.

34. Gillingham, *Richard the Lionheart*, p. 210.

35. Gillingham, *Richard the Lionheart*, p. 276.

36. Quoted in Regan, *Lionhearts*, p. 238.

Chapter 4: Saladin, Military Warrior

37. P.H. Newby, *Saladin in His Time*. London: Phoenix Press, 1983, p. 14.

38. Quoted in Newby, *Saladin in His Time*, p. 50.

39. Quoted in Newby, *Saladin in His Time*, p. 52.

40. Reston, *Warriors of God*, p. 6.

41. Quoted in Regan, *Lionhearts*, p. 41.

42. Newby, *Saladin in His Time*, p. 74.

43. Quoted in Newby, *Saladin in His Time*, p. 118.

44. Quoted in Newby, *Saladin in His Time*, p. 122.

45. Newby, *Saladin in His Time*, p. 158.

46. Regan, *Lionhearts*, p. 169.

47. Quoted in Newby, *Saladin in His Time*, p. 169.

48. Quoted in Regan, *Lionhearts*, p. 216.

49. Quoted from *The Crusades*, vol. 4: *Destruction*. BBC TV production in association with A&E Network, 1995.

Chapter 5: Don Pero Niño, Chivalrous Knight

50. D'A.J.D. Boulton, *The Knights of the Crown: The Monarchical Orders of Knighthood in Later Medieval Europe 1325–1520*. Suffolk, UK: Boydell Press, 2000, p. 61.

51. Boulton, *The Knights of the Crown*, p. 61.

52. Gutierre Diaz de Gamez, *The Unconquered Knight: A Chronicle of the Deeds of Don Pero Niño*. Translated by Joan Evans. New York: Brace, 1928, p. 33.

53. De Gamez, *The Unconquered Knight*, p. 36.

54. De Gamez, *The Unconquered Knight*, p. 37.

55. De Gamez, *The Unconquered Knight*, p. 65.

56. De Gamez, *The Unconquered Knight*, p. 73.

57. Hopkins, *Knights*, p. 153.

58. Quoted in de Gamez, *The Unconquered Knight*, p. 99.

59. De Gamez, *The Unconquered Knight*, p. 100.

60. Barber, *The Knight and Chivalry*, p. 151.

61. Barbara W. Tuchman, *A Distant Mirror: The Calamitous 14th Century*. New York: Ballantine Books, 1979, p. 448.

62. De Gamez, *The Unconquered Knight*, p. 148.

63. Quoted in de Gamez, *The Unconquered Knight*, p. 174.

64. Barber, *The Knight and Chivalry*, p. 151.

65. Quoted in de Gamez, *The Unconquered Knight*, p. 207.

Chapter 6: Bertrand du Guesclin, Soldier Knight

66. Hopkins, *Knights*, p. 160.

67. Barber, *The Knight and Chivalry*, p. 146.

68. Tim Newark, *Medieval Warlords*. Poole, UK: Blandford Press, 1987, p. 78.

69. Newark, *Medieval Warlords*, p. 79.

70. Quoted in Newark, *Medieval Warlords*, p. 82.

71. Newark, *Medieval Warlords*, pp. 82–83.

72. Quoted in Shirley N. Carr, *The King's Constable*. Richmond, VA: Garrett & Massie, 1951, p. 134.

73. Carr, *The King's Constable*, p. 168.

74. Quoted in Carr, *The King's Constable*, p. 182.

75. Quoted in Carr, *The King's Constable*, p. 183.

76. Quoted in Newark, *Medieval Warlords*, pp. 95–96.

77. Hopkins, *Knights*, p. 161.

78. Quoted in Newark, *Medieval Warlords*, pp. 97–99.

79. Quoted in Carr, *The King's Constable*, p. 241.

80. Quoted in Hopkins, *Knights*, p. 161.

81. Newark, *Medieval Warlords*, p. 101.

82. Hopkins, *Knights*, p. 161.

Chapter 7: Sir John de Hawkwood, Mercenary

83. Joseph Jay Deiss, *Captains of Fortune*. New York: Thomas Y. Crowell, 1967, p. 115.

84. Deiss, *Captains of Fortune*, p. 115.

85. Deiss, *Captains of Fortune*, p. 116.

86. Hopkins, *Knights*, p. 178.

87. Deiss, *Captains of Fortune*, p. 117.

88. Hopkins, *Knights*, p. 178.

89. Deiss, *Captains of Fortune*, p. 126.

90. Deiss, *Captains of Fortune*, p. 129.

91. Deiss, *Captains of Fortune*, p. 134.

92. Deiss, *Captains of Fortune*, p. 134.

93. Tuchman, *A Distant Mirror*, p. 322.

94. Deiss, *Captains of Fortune*, pp. 137–38.

95. Tuchman, *A Distant Mirror*, pp. 322–23.

96. Deiss, *Captains of Fortune*, p. 151.

For Further Reading

Michele Byam, *Arms and Armor*. New York: Dorling Kindersley, 2000. A photo essay examining the design, construction, and uses of hand weapons and armor.

Trevor Cairns, *Medieval Knights:* Cambridge, UK: Cambridge University Press, 1992. A good overview of medieval knights and their lives.

James A. Corrick, *Life of a Medieval Knight.* San Diego: Lucent Books, 2001. A comprehensive study of what life was like for a medieval knight, including training, armor, tournaments, and living in a manor.

Denise Dersin, ed., *What Life Was Like in the Age of Chivalry.* New York: Time-Life Books, 1997. An overview of medieval life from 800 to 1500 in Europe; includes a timeline from Roman rule to the Renaissance.

Amin Maalouf, *The Crusades Through Arab Eyes.* Translated by Jon Rothschild. New York: Schocken Books, 1985. A thought-provoking presentation of an Arab's viewpoint of the Crusades.

John Matthews, *Richard Lionheart: The Crusader King.* Dorset, UK: Firebird Books, 1988. A comprehensive but small book about Richard I; good for the young reader.

David Nicolle, *Medieval Knights.* New York: Viking, 1997. A pictorial book that covers the components of a knight's life.

Shelley Tanaka, *In the Time of Knights: The Real-Life Story of History's Greatest Knight.* New York: Hyperion, 2000. This book about William Marshal will appeal to young readers. The text reads like fiction and covers Marshal's life up until his journey to the Holy Land.

Myra Weatherley, *William Marshal: Medieval England's Greatest Knight.* Greensboro, NC: Morgan Reynolds, 2001. Well-organized book covering the major events of Marshal's life.

WORKS CONSULTED

Books

Richard Barber, *The Knight and Chivalry*. New York: Harper & Row, 1982. An excellent reference book on knights and chivalry.

D'A.J.D. Boulton, *The Knights of the Crown: The Monarchical Orders of Knighthood in Later Medieval Europe 1325–1520*. Suffolk, UK: Boydell Press, 2000. This book provides a scholarly survey of the late medieval monarchical orders of knighthood.

Shirley N. Carr, *The King's Constable*. Richmond, VA: Garrett & Massie, 1951. This book is very engaging, but since little is known of Bertrand du Guesclin's childhood, the author has taken some liberties with this period. However, after Guesclin received knighthood, Carr says, his career is a matter of record.

Gutierre Diaz de Gamez, *The Unconquered Knight: A Chronicle of the Deeds of Don Pero Niño*. Translated by Joan Evans. New York: Brace, 1928. Biography written by Pero Niño's flag bearer. Though it is obvious that de Gamez worshiped his master, the book remains one of the few surviving biographies of a medieval knight, and is the basis of much current study.

Joseph Jay Deiss, *Captains of Fortune*. New York: Thomas Y. Crowell, 1967. Very readable book that includes all major events in Hawkwood's life; covers other mercenaries as well.

Georges Duby, *William Marshal: The Flower of Chivalry*. Translated by Richard Howard. New York: Pantheon Books, 1985. Georges Duby is one of France's greatest medieval historians. This book on William Marshal is essential for any study of knights, and it reads easily.

John Gillingham, *Richard the Lionheart*. New York: Times Books, 1978. A thorough and detailed history of Richard I.

Andrea Hopkins, *Knights*. London: Quarto, 1990. A very useful overview of the knight that includes chronological tables of military and political history, art and literature, religion, and learning.

Tim Newark, *Medieval Warlords*. Poole, UK: Blandford Press, 1987. Describes the lives of seven warlords.

P.H. Newby, *Saladin in His Time*. London: Phoenix Press, 1983. A thorough and well-researched account of Saladin.

Sidney Painter, *William Marshal: Knight-Errant, Baron, and Regent of England*. Baltimore, MD: Johns Hopkins Press, 1933. The quintessential book on William Marshal, covering his life in great detail from beginning to end.

Geoffrey Regan, *Lionhearts*. New York: Walker, 1998. Alternates between Richard the Lionheart and Saladin as the key players in the Third Crusade.

James Reston Jr., *Warriors of God: Richard the Lionheart and Saladin in the Third Crusade*. New York: Doubleday, 2001. A dual biography of Richard the Lionheart and Saladin, bringing them face-to-face in the Third Crusade.

Georges Tate, *The Crusaders: Warriors of God*. New York: Harry N. Abrams, 1996. A very readable pocket guide that fully explains the Islamic world before the Crusades; the differences between the papacy in Rome and the Byzantine Empire in the East; and the First, Second, and Third Crusades. It also contains many paintings as well as an addendum of documents.

Barbara W. Tuchman, *A Distant Mirror: The Calamitous 14th Century*. New York: Ballantine Books, 1979. An in-depth study of the fourteenth century.

Videos

The Crusades. BBC TV production in association with A&E Network, 1995. Hosted by Terry Jones, this series of four videos is entertaining and humorously presented while maintaining integrity to the historical facts.

Picture Credits

About the Author

Janet R. Zohorsky has been a professional writer for six years. She has written for various regional magazines and newspapers on travel, lifestyles, and biographies. This is her first book. Her academic background includes master's and bachelor's degrees in English literature. Over the years, she has lived in Canada, Pennsylvania, California, Texas, and, most recently, Chicago, Illinois.